HOW TO RETIRE ON TIME

HOW TO
RETIRE
ON
TIME

CREATE A RETIREMENT PLAN DESIGNED TO LAST
LONGER THAN YOU

Mike Decker

How To Retire On Time

Create A Retirement Plan Designed To Last Longer Than You

Dedicated to Joan and Richard Urban,
my grandparents who spent their retirement helping raise me.
May they rest in peace.

And to my wife,
whom I love with all my heart.
May we continue to live our dreams.

"Wealth is the ability to fully experience life."
– Henry David Thoreau

CONTENTS

INTRODUCTION

HOW TO READ THIS BOOK

This book is written for two reasons.

Reason #1: So that you'll have more of your most precious commodity, time. I don't want you to work a day longer than necessary at a job you may not enjoy.

Reason #2: To first expose what are, in my opinion, oversimplified and risky retirement income strategies and second help you **create a retirement plan that is designed to last longer than you™ so you can retire on time** without fear of the next market crash or whatever else may cause you to delay your retirement or lose sleep.

I want to help you.

To do that, I've structured this book as follows:

Part 1 of this book is going to get heavy. I feel it would be a disservice if I didn't transparently and clearly share many of the potential problems you may face once you retire. To do that, we will need to break down some of the more popular retirement income strategies and their detriments.

Part 2 is focused on solutions. We will go through the process of designing what I call a Functional Wealth Plan™.

You may be asking, "What in the world is Functional Wealth™ of a Functional Wealth Plan™?" It's a phrase I started using some time ago that sums up how I believe all financial planning should be done. Functional Wealth™ was inspired by the functional doctors I have met over the years who continuously help people by using diet, exercise, and the use of both eastern and western medicine. I have no problem with the miracles that modern medicine gave to the world. I do believe that is important to look at the body as a whole, looking at the root cause of the problem, and not just addressing the symptoms.

That sums up how I believe financial planning should be done. Too often, plans are created with the intention of either trying to grow a portfolio fast enough that it somehow solves all your other problems, or trying to solve everything with a single product *cough* an income stream from an annuity *cough*. I'll explain later in the book why these strategies may be riskier than you realize, but for now please consider the fact that what you want is probably different than what many other people want, and it should be treated as such. There's no such thing as a perfect investment or a perfect investment strategy.

Functional Wealth™ suggests that what is right for one person or family may not be right for another person or family. It believes that you should not discuss or recommend strategies or products until you have at the very least a broad-based plan in place. That plan can offer you the context, clearly defining what you need and when you'll need it, so that you can have an educated conversation about investment products and strategies.

To go one step further, Functional Wealth™ also believes that you cannot create a broad-based plan unless you, and the advisor if you are getting help, have established what you want first. At the end of the day, your money is supposed to work for you in such a way that you are able to enjoy the life you want. It's all about you and how you want to spend your time, your most precious commodity. Here's the order, again:

Step 1: Determine the life you want to live.

Step 2: Create a plan that supports that vision.

Step 3: Implement strategies that make the plan possible.

For all intents and purposes, the plan that you will be able to create with this book will be a broad-based financial or retirement plan, not a comprehensive plan. Many people retire based on a broad-based retirement plan. However, creating a comprehensive plan requires a lot more back and forth than a book can offer. I hope you understand. If you don't understand the difference between a broad-based plan and a comprehensive plan, don't worry. You'll get a clear sense later in the book. Chances are, you'll be pleasantly surprised with how much financial clarity you can get from a broad-based plan, like the one you will create after going through this book.

On that note, please don't skip ahead. You may be tempted to just skip to the end and build your plan. **There are important principles and strategies you must understand before you start building your own retirement plan.** Don't put let yourself "put the cart before the horse," as they say. You must understand part one for part two to make sense.

When implemented correctly and properly funded, your Functional Wealth Plan™ should be designed to last longer than you, regardless of market conditions, tax rate changes, and so on.

For this to work, we will first put a preliminary plan together. The purpose is to "plan the gap." You may want to retire at 60 years old and file for Social Security at 67 years old. That leaves a seven-year gap. Those seven years will probably be your healthiest years in retirement. You should be traveling or spending your time doing what you love instead of living on a tight budget, or working longer than necessary, all because you are waiting for Social Security to start. Once we see what the plan could look like, and the potential gap within the plan, then we can start discussing which strategies could be implemented to help maximize your income overall.

It is so important to understand the sequence of retirement planning. Strategies support plans. Without a plan, your strategies have no context as to how they should be implemented or how they should operate. For example, you can talk all day long about IRA to Roth conversions. However, without a plan, it becomes extremely difficult to know how much to convert this year, how much to convert next year, what long-term effects could occur from those conversions, and so on. To implement strategies without a plan is putting the cart before the horse.

Once a plan is in place, we will review different strategies that you can consider implementing. The goal is to support the plan and ultimately your quality of life, regardless of whether markets go up, go down, or stay flat for 10 years or more.

Lastly, we will go through different scenarios to help make sure everything is working together in harmony. This will be your plan's stress test. **The goal is to give you the knowledge and tools so that by the end of the book, you'll be able to create a custom Functional Wealth Plan™ on your own (or with my team) and feel ready to retire on time with a retirement plan designed to last longer than you™.**

It might sound like a lot, but really, the entirety of this book can be summed up in the following three points:

Point #1: The volatility and uncertainty of the market and other financial factors cannot be controlled. Accepting what the markets can do is better than hoping for what we want them to do.

Point #2: Retirement income is the most important part of any plan. It must be consistent and flexible in order to sustain your lifestyle while keeping up with inflation.

Point #3: Those who are proactive in anticipating the ups and downs and planning accordingly can have a significant advantage over those who continue to invest as they have always invested and are in a reactive position. This book will show you how to put yourself and your wealth in a proactive position and help you design your retirement to last longer than you so you can enjoy the retirement you want. I call it a **Functional Wealth Plan™**.

The strategies you are about to learn have the potential to radically transform your life if implemented correctly. It may even help you retire sooner than expected.

They can also help you avoid retiring too soon and with the wrong plan. It's better to know now that you can't afford to retire instead of realizing later, like in your 80s, that you're going to run out of money and may need to go back to work. It's all based on achieving financial clarity with principle-based strategies structure, all guided by a broad-based plan.

My mission is to help as many people as I can enter retirement with adequate preparation and understanding so that once they retire, they can stay retired.

A mentor once told me years ago,

"If you start right, you can end right. If you start wrong, there's very little chance that you'll end right."

I want to help you start right. If you've already retired, but it has only been a few years, typically it's not too late to course-correct and get things on the right path if necessary.

If you read this book and decide you'd like help implementing its strategies as quickly as possible, please schedule a call to chat with me or my team by going here:

www.kedrec.com/call

Helping people like you retire on time is exactly what we do day-in and day-out.

We're here to help.

To your retirement success,

Mike Decker

Part 1

THE MODERN RETIREMENT

Chapter 1

THE RETIREMENT SHIFT

"Retirement, a time to do what you want to do, when you want to do it, where you want to do it, and, how you want to do it."

– Catherine Pulsifer

Before we get started, let me paint you a picture...

It's 2008.

You are grabbing lunch with an old friend at your favorite farm-to-table cafe. You get there early in your usual manner as you enjoy looking over the new items on the menu. Suddenly, you notice the presence of your friend, only there's something very different about him.

"What's wrong?" you ask.

"What do you mean what's wrong?! Everything's wrong! Markets are tanking. We're losing our retirement savings each day while my advisor keeps telling me to hang in there. My wife and I are looking for part-time work to help with the bills while we wait for our investments to recover. That's what's wrong. Have you been living under a rock these past few months?" he responds, exasperated.

You're not sure how to respond. Tomorrow, you're leaving for a three-week vacation to the Maldives. The retirement plan you built and the portfolio you have tell a different story.

You recall the conversations and planning you had in preparation for moments like this. From what you can tell, your investments and income are fine, even if the market turbulence continues for a few more years.

So, you respond with a few soundbites you heard on the news earlier that morning that focused on how bad things are and try to enjoy lunch with your friend.

The next day, you leave on your vacation, which becomes the three most incredible weeks of your life. As you head home, you notice that the markets have gone from bad to worse. Unemployment is now sky high. The government is issuing bailouts. With all the chaos, you look at your situation and confirm that you and your retirement are still in good order.

How is this possible?

For the record, this is a true account[1]. There really was a couple that, in spite of poor market conditions, still went on their vacation. I met them a few years after the 2008 financial crisis. When they told me their story, it changed my life. Their story is what inspired the research and development that would eventually turn into what you are now reading.

What you need to understand is I was taught what most of the industry teaches. "Put the majority of your assets in a stock/bond portfolio and take around 4% each year and you should be fine", they would say. Or "buy an annuity so you can get guaranteed income for life."

It was like all retirees had to pick from were two extremely different income strategies. Where was the balance or middle ground? Meeting this couple triggered the start of what has now become a life changing journey.

If nothing else, I hope that by the end of this book, you can understand what I was able to discover and consider it for your own retirement. I want to show you how to implement these principles and strategies so that you can design your retirement to last longer than you, even during difficult economic times. I want you to be able to enjoy your retirement similarly to how the couple in the story earlier were able to enjoy their retirement. Sure, your situation may be different, but I believe the rules and principles are the same.

It's worth mentioning, this couple did not have a pension. They did not have a dividend portfolio. They did not have a bunch of REITs (Real Estate Investment Trusts). They did not have any income streams from annuitized annuities. They did not have a generous executive retirement package.

They did what you will be learning in this book.

Over the past few decades, there has been a major shift in retirement planning. It used to be: work for 40 years, get the watch, and then live off the pension. Since the advent of the 401(k), pensions have mostly become a thing of the past. Now, whether you like it or not, the burden has been placed on your shoulders. Chances are, you are not a financial professional, which can make the entire endeavor feel overwhelming.

Because of the foresight and diligent preparation of this couple, when they woke up on the morning of their big retirement trip and saw the markets were tanking, they didn't panic. They had already planned for these situations. They knew where and how to pull income while markets were down—without compromising the integrity of their retirement. They could do this for years on end and wait out the recovery time.

I want that level of calmness and clarity for you. In this book, I'll share with you how they planned and the strategies they used. I also have several bonuses that can help you create your custom plan with ease. They range from access to my planning software (it's easy to use, even if you don't have a technical background) to on-demand courses and downloadable workbooks. The bonuses will dive deeper into topics like Social Security optimization, penson income vs. lump sum comparisons, and more, but more on that later. We're going to start with the fundamentals.

At this point, what's important to know is that there really isn't any special secret investment strategy or one perfect investment. That doesn't exist. The "secret," if that's what we're going to call it, is to properly understand how to plan and implement these strategies into a fluid framework that can adjust to whatever happens in the future. It's all about understanding and following principles, universal truths that can help guide you in your unique situation.

You can plan all you want, but when the market moves one way or another, your plan becomes inaccurate. No one has a crystal ball, which is why it is so important to have a general direction, supported by strategies that are fluid enough to adjust along the way. In my opinion (and based on my research), when you follow what you are about to learn, you can significantly increase your probability of success in retirement.

This framework can apply even if you want to self-manage your investments and retirement. You probably didn't expect me to admit to that, but it is absolutely true. If you wanted, I'm confident that you could design, build, and maintain your retirement just by reading this book and implementing these strategies into your plan.

I won't give client testimonials in this book. Confidentiality is everything, especially in the financial industry. However, I want to run through a few hypothetical situations with you to help illustrate how the process is intended to work.

"I LOST MY JOB A FEW YEARS BEFORE I WANTED TO RETIRE"

Regardless of the reason, whether it's a bad economy, office politics, or something else, losing your job is typically a surprise. Going back to the job market right before you want to retire can be very stressful. What do you say in the interview? "Hey, I want a job for a year or so and then I'm out?" I know it may not be politically correct to say, but the elephant is in the room, whether people admit it or not.

Let's say you are 64 years old, and you are planning to retire at the age of 67 so you can time it with when you file for Social Security. And then one day, you unexpectedly lose your job. Let's also assume that you believe you have not saved enough to be able to retire. You may not have created an actual plan, but you've read enough to know what your number probably is. What do you do?

First off, don't assume anything. Until you create a plan, like you are about to do in this book, you really don't have enough context to determine if you can retire or not. You may be able to retire right now. It just depends on how much income you want and how much you have saved.

Second, a common assumption is that you should file for Social Security when you retire. It's just not true. You can design your Functional Wealth Plan™ to provide a smooth overall income stream while bridging the gap between when you retire and when you file for Social Security. This process will also teach you how to do that.

Regardless of how far away your target retirement date is, go through this process. You may discover that you could potentially retire sooner than expected. In Part 2 of the book, I'm going to walk you through how to create a Functional Wealth Plan™, which is a broad-based retirement plan that can help you see if you can afford to retire today, or not. If not today, then it can show you when you can afford to retire. You never know, your results may surprise you.

Don't worry if you are not tech savvy. What I will show you is easier to do than you may think. At that point, it will be up to you if you decide to retire sooner or later but knowing that you could retire sooner if you had to has its benefits.

"I CAN'T RETIRE UNTIL MEDICARE STARTS"

How much is a year of your life worth? That might seem like a strange question, but when people come in and tell me they can't retire until Medicare starts, that's the first thing I ask.

The average monthly cost for an HMO plan for a 60-year-old is around $930 per month or $11,160 per year. That breaks down to around $30 per day.

Let's say you and your spouse are 63 years old. Do you love your job? Would you do it, even if you were not paid? If yes, then it may not make sense to retire. But if given the chance, you'd quit today, then consider the price of your time.

Each year you spend, working at a job you hate, you are essentially giving up your time to save around $11,160 per year (or whatever the rate would be for you). Or, you could pay around $30 per day and have 365 days to do what you want with your precious time.

They say time is money. I say money is time saved with the intention of spending it later at your discretion so you can enjoy the life you want. If you are unwilling to spend your money to enjoy your time now, then when?

In Chapter 6, I will be showing you how to plan for the pre-Medicare gap so that you can potentially retire sooner without compromising your overall retirement. Even if you can afford to retire before Medicare starts, you may decide to keep working anyway. If that's what you want, it's still considered a win. It's all about you spending your time how you want to spend it.

"I HAVE A 401(K) BUT DON'T KNOW WHAT TO DO WITH IT"

It's easy to do what you have always done. Chances are, you've become comfortable with buying and holding mutual funds. You've probably done that for years in your 401(k). But what you did to get to this point may not be what you need to do in order to get to where you want to go. Once you stop getting a paycheck from an employer and start paying yourself from your savings, there's an additional amount of responsibility placed on your investments.

Let's say you have a 401(k) with a sufficient amount in it for retirement. You could keep it in mutual funds and ride the markets up and down. Many people find that stressful, so they look for other options. You've probably considered diversifying into CDs, annuities, and so on. Sound familiar?

Notice the lack of direction. How do you know if you should get a CD? Is it to have less risk? How do you know you need less risk? Was it a gut feeling? When will you use that CD for income? What about your mutual funds? Do you time the market on when to sell each fund? You can see where I am going with this.

Later in the book, I'm going to teach you my three retirement principles: the Principle of Income, the Principle of Diversification, and the Principle of Planning. Together, they can help you gain context and direction on what you may want to do with your 401(k). Unless you have a plan, or understand these principles, it can be hard to know what to do with your 401(k) and other investments.

In Chapter 7, I'm going to explore different ways you can deliberately design your portfolio to support your plan. Instead of investment ambiguity, basically a pie chart that is supposed to grow and solve all your problems, we are going to give context to each year of the plan and create multiple strategies to help you keep income coming in, regardless of market conditions. We will be assigning purpose to each investment and or product, so you can potentially enjoy more financial clarity and ultimately a newfound sense of calmness throughout retirement.

The process you are about to take can help you determine what you should do with your 401(k) and other investments. It all revolves around your plan. Once completed, your plan can help you diversify by objectives, instead of trying to manage a portfolio full of ambiguity.

"I WANT TO TRAVEL BUT MY CURRENT PLAN IS HOLDING ME BACK"

Let's say you can afford to retire at 60 years old and want to travel as much as you can until the age of 65. How do you do it without compromising your overall plan? What if the markets crashed during your first few years in retirement? Would you just cancel your trips and sit around the house until things recover? That doesn't sound like a dream come true.

Spending too much too soon is a common concern. As you go through this book and the overall process, you will learn techniques and strategies that can help you front load your plan with income so you can travel while potentially lowering your overall risk during those travel years, just in case the markets do crash.

I'm going to teach you about an income strategy called, The Principal Guaranteed Reservoir™, which can help you increase your growth potential while minimizing your overall risk and maintaining a reasonable amount of liquidity and flexibility within your portfolio. This strategy challenges your traditional stock/bond portfolio and annuitized, "guaranteed for life" income stream, which are two of the more common retirement income strategies.

In addition, in Chapter 8, I'm going to walk you through how to use the Principal Guaranteed Reservoir™ in conjunction with other various income and growth strategies to help keep income coming in regardless of market conditions. Basically, I not only want to help you create a retirement plan that is designed to last longer than you™, but I also want to help you learn how to manage it on your own. I want to teach you how to fish, as they say.

When I said I honestly want to help you design your retirement to last longer than you, I really meant it. I'm okay if you don't want to become a client of mine at Kedrec. However, I'm not okay with the thought that your retirement could be compromised because you did not follow the principles I am about to share. I want you to be successful.

The purpose of a Functional Wealth Plan™ is to give you financial context so you can coordinate the multiple strategies needed in order to help you retire with the highest probability of success. Period. Even if you've already retired, you can still make the necessary adjustments and develop your own Functional Wealth Plan™.

To be completely frank, most people we work with have already retired. At some point, they become nervous and ask us to help them "fix" their retirement before it's too late. If that's you, don't worry. Just keep reading.

Wherever you are in the retirement process, this book is meant to give you a very clear picture of how to retire and stay retired.

So, if you're ready to learn ways to help you lower your risk, possibly increase your income, maybe even retire a couple of years before you would have normally expected, and set yourself up for success with a Functional Wealth Plan™, then I'll see you in the next chapter.

Chapter 2

WHO THIS BOOK IS FOR

"Often when you think you're at the end of something, you're at the beginning of something else."

– Fred Rogers

The strategies you are about to learn come from a decade of frustration with the financial services industry. No matter where I looked, all I could find were oversimplified sales pitches that ignored the downside of the "solution" being presented.

I've met with too many people who locked up all of their assets in privately held REITs that stopped paying the expected dividend (income). Then when they tried to sell them, no one wanted to buy them.

There have been too many people who planned their retirement with insurance agents who locked up too much in income annuities. When inflation went up, they could not afford to maintain their quality of life.

On the other side of the industry, I've seen too many retirees have a "diversified portfolio" that lost a significant amount of money when the markets went down. They were all at risk because that is what they were used to in years past. They withdrew income from their accounts when they were down, accentuating their losses and compromising their overall retirement.

My frustration didn't just come from people coming into my office with problems caused by others within the industry. It also came from many sleepless nights with my own clients. My lack of sleep wasn't derived from concern about my client accounts and how the stock market was acting, or how inflation was going to affect my clients' ability to afford their lifestyle. We had planned for those situations, which you will learn about in this book.

I was losing sleep over the illusion of choice clients had. It felt like we were creating co-dependent relationships. "You need us or else…" seemed to be the theme. It didn't sit well with me. The reality is, back in the 70s, you probably did need a financial professional if you wanted to invest in the market, and so on. However, today you can manage your portfolio on your phone while you are on the beach in Italy. Many people will take the standard deduction when they file for taxes, making Turbo Tax® or other solutions like it a wonderful and affordable option.

In my mind, the reality was people just needed help putting together a retirement plan. That way, they could get answers to the questions they didn't know to ask. However, once it was set up and correctly funded, it felt like they really didn't need us anymore. It was almost like we were getting a residual income because we set it up and appeared to be the expert, even though in many situations, they probably could have done it on their own.

Would you pay a residual to the builder of your home because they did a good job building it? Absolutely not. Then why are people paying so much money every year for a service that they could probably do on their own?

"It's the way it has always been done," advisors would say.

It just didn't sit right with me.

This book, these strategies I am going to show you, and more, are all to help you become financially independent, including independence from your advisor. I don't believe in co-dependent relationships. I want you to finish this book knowing you have three options.

First, you could walk away with enough information to put a plan together and manage it on your own without paying an advisor a dime. Second, you may walk away with enough information to put a plan together and manage it on your own, but you want some of your assets actively managed (i.e., Absolute Return models or Probability Investment Models™). If that's you, great. The point is, you made the decision because you wanted it, not because you needed it. Lastly, you may want a family office like experience. Basically, you want access to a financial advisor, CPA, insurance agent, and more, who all work together in harmony. If that is you, no problem, that is possible as well.

The point is, you should be able to get the financial guidance you need and want while being supported with the outcome you desire. No more takeaway closes and manipulative sales pitches claiming that "you need us or else you're at risk." In my opinion, it's just not true.

Based on my experience, most of the time people are doing many things right. The problem is there are one or two big blind spots that leave them exposed to more risk than they realize. It's true that one or two big blind spots could compromise someone's entire retirement. However, that doesn't mean you need a life-long co-dependent relationship.

Yes, sometimes it takes a professional to come in, point out the potential problem, and then recommend strategies to help alleviate it. However, once the awareness is raised, and you've "learned how to fish," there's a good chance you can maintain your plan on your own.

You can't solve problems you don't know exist. I want to point out those common blind spots. I want to show you the principles that can help you address those blind spots and potentially lower your overall risk. What I am going to show you is not common. You're probably not going to get it from any of the large brokerage houses or the strip mall advisors down the road. It's not fancy or incredibly technical. In fact, I believe that because it is so simple, many miss it.

During our time together, not only are you going to learn several uncommon strategies, like the Principal Guaranteed Reservoir™, but you are also going to be able to mathematically determine if you can afford to retire today or not. Can you imagine what that would look like? You may discover that you could retire today if you wanted.

I do want to point out that just because you may be able to retire today, or next year, or whenever your projections suggest, that doesn't mean you have to retire then. It all boils down to being prepared so that you can retire when you want, if you want.

My goal is not only to help you retire on time but also to help you sleep better at night, even when the markets are going down. Retirement should not be financially stressful. Once you build a plan you understand, it should take very little time to maintain, leaving you with more time to spend on other activities.

They say that people spend more time planning their vacations each year than managing their finances. I hope that is your retirement experience. I hope that your retirement is full of time with family and friends, enjoying bucket list trips and backyard BBQs. You spent your entire life working, saving, and investing, so you can enjoy this special season.

It is my sincere hope that by showing you how to create a Functional Wealth Plan™, you may be able to retire on time with a plan designed to last longer than you so that you can spend your time where it matters most.

This book is for anyone who:

- Wants to retire within the next 10 years.
- Has already retired and is uncomfortable with their current plan and/or strategies.
- Wants to lower their overall risk.
- Wants to increase their long-term growth potential.
- Wants to fire their advisor and manage their plan on their own.
- Wants to manage their plan on their own but doesn't know the right questions to ask.
- Wants to retire as soon as possible.
- Wants to diversify their portfolio outside of the stock/ bond market.

- Wants to understand and optimize their Social Security income.
- Wants to proactively minimize their taxes without compromising their income or portfolio so they can pass their assets tax-efficiently to their beneficiaries.
- Has a pension and wants to compare their pension option to their lump sum option.
- Has rental real estate and wants to spend less time being a landlord.

Key Chapter Takeaways

- There is no such thing as a perfect investment or a perfect investment strategy. It takes deliberate proactive steps toward clear expectations in order to retire on time with a plan that is designed to last longer than you.

- Just because you can retire, doesn't mean you have to retire. The goal is to gain clarity, so you have more control over how you spend your time, whether that is at the office or somewhere else.

- You've worked and saved your entire life for the ability to retire and enjoy a certain quality of life. By following the principles and rules shared within this book, and by creating a Functional Wealth Plan™, you may be able to fulfill your retirement expectations. It's time to take deliberate steps toward your dreams so that they can become a reality.

Chapter 3

PROBLEMS WITH COMMON INCOME STRATEGIES

"It ain't what you don't know that gets you into trouble. It's what you know for sure that just ain't so."

– Mark Twain

I've been fortunate to be the keynote speaker at several conferences and conduct workshops as a national coach to other financial advisors. In addition, I've been privileged to spend time visiting with some of the brightest minds on Wall Street.

I share all of that for one reason.

In my experience, research, and discussions with other high-profile financial professionals, I've learned a few things. These are things you can only learn if someone goes out of their way to show you. They are not obvious, but once you see it, you can't unsee it (in a good way).

Please take my experience and research and embrace the reality of these popular retirement income strategies so:

1) you don't have to learn the hard way with your own retirement.

2) you can become obsessed with your retirement, these principles, and framework found within this book like I have.

Chances are, you've created a plan around one of the strategies I outline below. If you have, then I'm asking you to please keep an open mind. Changing strategies can feel hard, especially with so much at stake. But, at the end of the day, all I want is for you to have all the right information.

The reality is, if these common retirement income strategies were as good as people claim, I'd be recommending them myself. I've seen too much to stay silent. It's why I wrote this book. I want to help you. That includes helping you not get blindsided by the risks of these popular retirement income strategies.

If you'll allow me to explain these strategies and their risks, I promise to show you how I design people's retirement plans to last longer than them with portfolios that offer a blend of growth potential, principal protection, and liquidity.

Now, it's possible that one of the strategies I will be discussing happens to be your current strategy. Please keep an open mind as my intention is not to criticize you. My purpose is to help you see the risks you may be taking while helping you consider a different way to manage your retirement and portfolio. When implemented correctly, these strategies may be able to help you increase your long-term growth potential while lowering your overall risk. It's not about "who is right." I want to focus on "what is right." I promise to show you the light by the time you finish this book so you can walk away feeling excited about your future.

Are you ready?

Let's begin.

COMMON INCOME STRATEGY #1: THE 4% RULE

One of the more common retirement income strategies is called the 4% rule. The idea is that if stocks average around 7%–8% year over year and if your bonds and bond funds average around 3%–4% year over year, you could take 4% of your portfolio as retirement income and be fine. Seems easy enough, right?

What makes this strategy more appealing is it's probably similar to what you've been doing for years. Plus, it offers more growth potential and flexibility than other common retirement income strategies. Who doesn't love growth and flexibility?

The problem can be found in something called *sequence of returns risk*, which suggests that when it comes to dollars and cents, the sequence of the return matters. There are two major problems when you consider this risk. The first is the deception behind return averages. For example, did you know that it is possible for your account to grow faster with a 6% average return than an 8% average return? Here's how that works.

Say you invest $100,000 in the market. In year one, the market gets hit hard and you get a -30% return on your investment, leaving you with $70,000. In year two, the market recovers and you get a 19% return, leaving you with $83,300. In year three, the market takes off and you get a return of 35%, leaving your account with $112,455.

The average return based on the annual performance is 8% (-30, 19%, and 35%). However, the three-year return based on the ending cash value is around 12.46%. Now divide that by three and you get an average return, based on the ending cash value, of 4.15% per year. Eight percent is very different than 4.15%.

Now, let's run it again. Say you invest $100,000 in the market. In year one, you get a return on your investments of 7%, leaving you with $107,000. In year two, you get a return on your investments of 5%, leaving you with $112,350. In year three, you get a return on your investments of 6% again, leaving your account with $119,091.

The average return based on the annual performance is 6% (7%, 5%, and 6%). However, the three-year return based on the ending cash value is around 19.09%. Now divide that by the three years and you get a 6.36% return per year. It doesn't seem like it should be this way, but it's hard to argue with math.

Consider the following. If you were to lose 10% in your portfolio, it would take an 11% gain to break even, not 10%. A 1% difference is not huge. However, if you were to lose 30% in your portfolio, you would need a 43% gain to recover. The deeper you dig, the harder it is to get out.

Now imagine you are retired, and the markets crashed. Your portfolio takes a 30% hit. You still need your income, so you take out around 4% of your assets as income. You are now down 34%. It will now take a 50% return just to break even.

Instead of leaving your losses at a negative 30%, requiring a 43% gain to break even, you accentuate your losses to 34%, requiring a 50% gain just to break even. That's an additional 7% gain you now need because you took income from an account that had already lost money.

The big takeaway here is in retirement, avoiding the losses can make a huge difference. The reason why the 8% return did worse than the 6% return is because it took a major loss in the first year. To put that into perspective, those who retire and keep most all their investment in a stock/bond portfolio and then experience a market crash early on in their retirement are mathematically at a disadvantage.

It can take years to recover from a market crash. Investors can have short term memories, which can expose us to an unnecessary amount of risk. We won't go too deep into detail here, but consider the following historical market data and its patterns. Even though market performance cannot be predicted or assured in the future, it is interesting to consider the following:

- The markets historically tended to correct (-10% or so) every 1.8 years[2]
- The markets historically tended to crash (-30% or more) every 7–8 years[3]
- The markets historically tended to go flat every 18 years or so[4]

If you take nothing else from this book, I hope you understand this important point. How and when you draw your retirement income matters.

One of the three retirement principles we will be discussing in this book is called the Principle of Income, which suggests that you only draw income from accounts that have not received significant losses. Failing to do so may have negative effects on your income and assets and may ultimately compromise your retirement.

Now imagine for a moment if you were able to pull income from an account that hadn't lost anything during a market crash. This problem essentially goes away, right? The solution is simpler than you may realize. I'll show you how to do that later in the book.

For now, take a moment and check in with yourself. If you can't say yes to the following questions, you could be taking more risk than you realize.

SUCCESS CHECK-IN EXERCISE

Before we proceed with the rest of the book, let's first check in with where you are right now with your retirement preparations. You can still complete the check-in if you are currently retired.

Below, rate yourself on a scale from 0–5 on how accurate the statements are—0 means "not accurate at all," and 5 means "most accurate."

Once you've rated yourself for each statement, total up your scores and then use the Answer Key to determine your next steps.

Success Check-in Statement	Self-Rating
I know how much income I can afford to take this year and not run out of money.	
I know how much income I can afford to take in five years and not run out of money.	
If the markets were to crash next year, I could pull enough income from my assets without accentuating any losses.	
If the markets were to crash in five years, I could pull enough income from my assets without accentuating any losses.	
I am prepared for three to four significant market crashes in retirement.	
I am prepared for a potential ten-year period of no returns in retirement.	
Market conditions will not affect my lifestyle or travel plans.	

WHAT YOUR SCORE REALLY MEANS

SCORE: 0–28
HOW THINGS HAVE ALWAYS BEEN DONE COULD HURT YOU

If you ended up here, chances are you haven't retired yet or you kept investing the same way you have always invested.

You may think that the upside potential and good years will offset the down years. That may be true, but only if you do not touch it.

When you retire, you need to be able to generate income. Hopefully, the pages of this book will show you that you don't need to take that much risk. You don't need to be the richest person in the graveyard. It's all about time and how you want to spend it. Please commit to finishing the book and keeping an open mind. You may be surprised at what you find.

SCORE: 29–31
EVERYTHING IN LIFE IS A TRADE

If your score landed you here, chances are you are still holding on to something. Maybe it is hope for a good year to make up for past losses. Maybe you want to prove to yourself that you are an intelligent and successful investor. Whatever it is, let it go.

You don't want to retire from retirement and have to go back to work. There's no such thing as a perfect investment. There's no such thing as a perfect investment strategy. The Functional Wealth Plan™ could be the missing piece to help you shore up your current plan and supporting strategies. Even if you don't like what you read today, the fact remains, there are some areas that need attention and possible adjustments.

SCORE: 32+
TIME TO ENHANCE YOUR PLAN

You've done your research and you've got a plan for every possible outcome. You're confident in your strategies and are sleeping well at night. There's just one problem: You've hit the limit of your own abilities.

It's time to take your plan to the next level. Whether that is doing a deep dive into tax minimization strategies, or optimizing your growth potential overall, there's still a lot you could learn from this book. By the end of the book, you will discover additional products and investments, and their underlying strategies that you often can't get as a retail investor. I'll show you where to go to get them and how you could consider them in your plan.

POPULAR INCOME STRATEGY #2: THE ANNUITIZED INCOME STREAM

When someone realizes the amount of risk a stock/bond portfolio has in their retirement income, and how taking income from accounts that have lost money can be detrimental, they might start panicking. "What else can I do to ensure my retirement will last?" This is where insurance agents often come in and offer "guaranteed income for life."

They may say something like, "Imagine an investment that grows with the market without any risk of losing money. When you are ready, you can turn on your income, which is guaranteed for life!" Sometimes, agents will offer an income annuity with a special lump sum bonus to kick-start your retirement savings. Sounds like free money, right? Are you getting suspicious?

The sales pitch doesn't stop there. Sometimes, prospective clients are promised that the income annuity is guaranteed to grow by at least 15% every year until you start your lifetime income. If the market averages 7%–8% each year, you'd be stupid not to lock in such a fantastic rate, right?

Can you feel your stomach starting to turn, yet? If it sounds too good to be true, it usually is. Here's what they are actually selling…

If you calculate your lifetime income amount's average rate of return based on the cash surrender value (not the annuity contract value or income benefit value), you may be disappointed. Once you start taking income under the annuitization option, you can no longer cancel the annuity for cash and get the lump sum of money back. **The choice to annuitize is irrevocable.**

Why does this matter? Inflation. If inflation outpaces your annuitized income stream, then you could be losing your ability to sustain your quality of life. This is called purchase power risk.

Imagine trying to live today based on wages of 10–20 years ago. It'd be tough, right? Now imagine agreeing to a lifetime wage 20 years ago. Once started, that wage could not be negotiated. Would you have got it right? It's hard to imagine, even after living through it, how much the world has changed in the last 20 to 30 years. Imagine what things will be like 20 years from now.

The lack of flexibility once the income stream is turned on is concerning. At this point, if you have annuities, you may be upset and want to put this book down and review those accounts. If you have one (or several), continue reading. After the check-in assessment, I'll walk you through how to better vet your annuities.

Whatever the results are, please promise me you will finish the book. We are still going through the other problems with popular income strategies. In Part 2, we'll walk through how to find solutions. I want to show you how you can benefit from the financial assurance these annuities can offer without locking up the assets for life.

I hope that as you review your annuities, they turn out to be better than expected. If not, don't panic. There may be ways to fix or adjust them. We just need to take this one step at a time.

I'll see you in the next section.

SUCCESS CHECK-IN EXERCISE

Before we proceed with the rest of the book, let's first check in with where you are right now with your retirement preparations. You can still complete the check-in if you are currently retired.

Below, rate yourself on a scale from 0–5 on how accurate the statements are—0 means "not accurate at all," and 5 means "most accurate."

Once you've rated yourself for each statement, total up your scores and then use the Answer Key to determine your next steps.

Success Check-in Statement	Self-Rating
I have flexibility with my investments and products.	
My retirement income is expected to keep up with inflation.	

All of my investments and products, based on their cash value, are growing at a reasonable rate.

If markets were to crash and I didn't want to pull income from my accounts that have lost money, I would still have enough liquidity to handle a major life event, like a new roof or car.

I have a comprehensive plan that dictates what investments and products I should have and how I should use them. (Basically, I did not just buy an annuity to solve everything)

I understand how my investments and products work.

I understand and am comfortable with the fees associated with my investments and products.

WHAT YOUR SCORE REALLY MEANS

SCORE: 0–28
FIXING CAN BE PAINFUL

Whether you've got fees that are too high, not enough liquidity, investments are not staying competitive, or something else, addressing it and fixing it can be painful. That doesn't mean that you surrender your annuities, liquidate your stocks, and start all over. It means the best thing to do is keep reading and see how you can slowly and deliberately transition from where you are now to where you want to be.

As you read the book, imagine that you've got complete freedom to invest however you want. Once you finish putting your plan together, then you can start working backward so you can figure out what needs to be done every step of the way. You got this.

SCORE: 29–31
A FEW ADJUSTMENTS WON'T HURT

You're likely only a few adjustments away from the retirement you want. There are probably a few investments or products you want to sell so you can move on to bigger and better things.

The good news is you probably have a good foundation. Now it's time to work on some renovation. As you continue to read, consider what the book proposes and how it may be able to further enhance your overall retirement and potentially help you reach your financial goals faster.

SCORE: 32+
TIME TO ORGANIZE

Chances are, you've got the right investments and products. It is now time to potentially make a few adjustments to try and get more out of them. Where and how to pull income can take a lot of planning upfront. Once everything is set correctly, it can be very easy to manage.

As you read the rest of the book, pay attention to the protocols and strategies. They may be able to help you get more out of your investments and products as you continue through retirement.

SELF-GUIDED ANNUITY REVIEW

If you have an income annuity, call the insurance company directly and ask them these questions to determine if it makes sense for you to keep your annuity or to look for other options.

What type of annuity is this? (circle one)
- ☐ Income Annuity - SPIA (focused on guaranteed income for life)
- ☐ Fixed Annuity with Rider (focused on guaranteed income for life)
- ☐ Fixed Annuity (fixed interest, principal protected)
- ☐ Fixed-Indexed Annuity (variable growth potential, principal protected)
- ☐ Variable Annuity (variable growth potential, not principal protected)

How much was originally invested?

_____

What is the current cash surrender value?

_____

What is the average annual return based on the initial cash value?

_____

What fees, if any, are deducted directly from my annuity value?

_____

How long until I can liquidate my annuity without a surrender penalty?

_____

Please note that as you assess your annuity, remember that all annuity withdrawals are subject to ordinary income taxes, as well as a 10% federal penalty if a distribution is taken out before the age of 59 ½.

There are a lot more questions that could be asked, but they go down a few rabbit holes. This should get you started in discovering if your annuity is doing what you had originally hoped for, or not.

POPULAR INCOME STRATEGY #3: THE PENSION

If you have the fortune of being offered a pension, consider yourself blessed. They are getting more and more rare. However, everything, including pensions, has its benefits and its detriments. While the benefit of getting lifetime income sounds nice, there are a few things to consider.

First, make sure the pension plan is well funded. You do not want your pension going away because of poor business decisions by your employer. It is rare, but it does happen from time to time.

Second, consider the effect that taxes could have on your pension. Since pensions are taxed as ordinary income, if taxes go up, your net income goes down. No one can know the future of taxes, so you'll need to consider what you expect will happen with future tax rates and then plan accordingly.

Third, a pension can forfeit any possible benefits to your kids. If you were to take the pension and then pass sooner than expected, it's all gone. Depending on your financial goals, that could make a difference.

All that said, pension income streams are more often elected over the lump sum. Why? I believe it is because pensions are considered less risky than the market and tend to offer a more competitive income stream than if you were to put it into an annuity and annuitize it.

I don't want to discourage you from electing to take the pension. However, later in the book, I'm going to show you how to compare your pension option to the lump sum option. I want to show you what it could look like if you were to take the lump sum and slowly convert it from pre-tax dollars to tax-free dollars for two reasons. One, you will probably need it for income. These types of conversions can help lower future tax liabilities. Two, to pass on assets more efficiently to your heirs.

The choice is yours to make. My job is to explain the risks and compare your options so you can make the best decision possible for your unique situation. If you have a pension, then please do this quick Success Check-in Exercise. If not, just skip it.

SUCCESS CHECK-IN EXERCISE

Below, rate yourself on a scale from 0–5 on how accurate the statements are—0 means "not accurate at all," and 5 means "most accurate."

Once you've rated yourself for each statement, total up your scores and then use the Answer Key to determine your next steps.

Success Check-in Statement	Self-Rating
Income stability is more important to me than leaving a large sum to my kids and grandkids.	
If I (and my spouse, if applicable), were to pass a few years into retirement, I would not roll over in my grave from all the potential money that could have gone to the kids and grandkids.	
I want the least amount of market risk possible without compromising my retirement.	
I am in good health and expect to live past 85 years old.	

I am not concerned about future tax rates.

I am not concerned about future cost of living increases due to inflation.

I expect my lifestyle and basic living expenses to slowly go down over time as I slow down my activities in retirement.

WHAT YOUR SCORE REALLY MEANS

SCORE: 0-19
CONSIDER THE LUMP SUM OPTION

Maybe you don't expect to live as long as others. You might be concerned about inflation, taxes, and other future potential problems, or you would prefer to have more control over your destiny. If those things are true, the lump sum option may be in your best interest.

Though this result is not a definitive answer to your choice between a pension and a lump sum, consider what it would look like if you did take the lump sum option and manage your retirement and portfolio based on the strategies explained in this book.

In Part 2 of the book, I'm going to take you through an exercise that will either help you have more confidence in taking the lump sum option or convince you to take the pension as an income stream. There are many factors at play that we'll address head-on.

SCORE: 20+
CONSIDER THE PENSION INCOME OPTION

Maybe you expect to live a long time, or you just can't handle market fluctuations. If your score puts you in the pension income camp, there's a good chance that no matter what this book says, your best bet might be to take the pension income stream.

The art of financial planning comes into play when you consider a person's emotional preference (what they can handle and what they cannot handle on a day-to-day basis). The number one goal for most people is to retire and stay retired. If your answers brought you here, chances are that your pension's income option may be the better option for you. From this point on, read the book with the assumption that you will take the pension as income vs. a lump sum and everything else is intended to support you and your pension. Remember, we are focused on "what is right," and not "who is right." Your friends and colleagues are not you. This is all about you and your retirement success, financially and emotionally.

In Part 2, I'm going to walk you through how to compare your different pension income options. For some, you'll have different pension income start dates. In my opinion, you should retire when you want, not when the pension income says. I'm going to show you how you can set your own retirement date, bridge the income gap, and take the pension income option that is best suited for you.

POPULAR INCOME STRATEGY #4: THE DIVIDEND PORTFOLIO

Let's start with a simple question. If I could offer you a 2% annual dividend, would you take it?

How about a 5% dividend?

7%? 10%? 15%?

How about a 42% annual dividend? Would you take it?

At some point, you've got to wonder how much risk is behind the investment and their ability to pay the dividends. That is the root of the problem behind a dividend income strategy. For the record, I did see a 42% annual dividend once. It was an extremely high-risk situation. If memory serves me well, that dividend didn't last very long.

According to many financial experts, your basic dividend portfolio should expect around 1%–6% return as annual income, based on its value each year. Those dividends are not guaranteed. If times are tough, dividends can be under pressure. If interest rates go up, like bonds, dividend-paying stocks can find themselves under pressure as well, which could mean they lose value.

Typically, value stocks, which pay dividends, grow at slower rates than balanced or growth stocks. If you were to reinvest the dividends, you may be able to rationalize a more competitive return on investment. However, you can't have your cake and eat it too. You either reinvest the dividend or you spend it. If you spend it, it can become more difficult for your investments to keep up with inflation.

In addition to the pressure of performance and interest rate risk, dividend portfolios are still considered at risk. They can lose value, which puts pressure on the income you need. If you have to sell stocks to keep income coming in, you would be accentuating your losses, ultimately making matters worse.

The idea is well-intended. Buy good stocks that pay good dividends. The stocks may fluctuate, but the dividend should hopefully pay at around the same. The problem is there isn't much of a backup plan. If the dividends stop, what's plan B? Sell some of your stock or mutual fund positions? That compromises your long-term ability to maintain your income.

In addition to the lack of a backup plan, it can be difficult, if not impossible to bridge any gap. If you want to retire at 60 and take your Social Security at 67, your dividend portfolio doesn't care. They will pay what they pay. That means during your potentially healthiest years in retirement, you are on a tighter than necessary budget while you wait for Social Security to kick in. The alternative may be to keep working longer than you need, which may not be how you want to spend your time.

Later in the book, I want to show you how you can pull income from your portfolio, based on your plan, while still being cognizant of your overall account balance. If you want to maintain your principal, no problem. If you want to spend down principal, that's okay too. The goal is to take more control over when, where, and how you get your income so you don't leave it up to the whims of the businesses and hope they pay enough dividends to sustain yourself. There are things we cannot control and there are things we can control. Let's give you as much control as is reasonably possible.

SUCCESS CHECK-IN EXERCISE

Before we proceed with the rest of the book, let's first check in with where you are right now with your retirement preparations. You can still complete the check-in if you are currently retired.

Below, rate yourself on a scale from 0–5 on how accurate the statements are—0 means "not accurate at all," and 5 means "most accurate."

Once you've rated yourself for each statement, total up your scores and then use the Answer Key to determine your next steps.

Success Check-in Statement	Self-Rating
If markets went up, I know where and how I would pull my income without accentuating losses or compromising my portfolio.	
If markets went down, I know where and how I would pull my income without accentuating losses or compromising my portfolio.	
If markets went flat, I know where and how I would pull my income without accentuating losses or compromising my portfolio.	
I am not dependent on any particular business and their ability to make a profit.	
I am aware of the risks behind each of my investments.	

I understand how to bridge my income gap between when I retire and when my income streams start, like Social Security.

I am deliberately diversified among different investment and product types, indexes, and sectors.

WHAT YOUR SCORE REALLY MEANS

SCORE: 0-28
IT'S TIME TO MOVE INTO A MORE PROACTIVE POSITION

It's time to stop letting the whims of the market control your life. There are things you cannot control. However, you can control the design of your plan and its supporting strategies.

Your next steps, as you continue to read, must be focused on asking yourself, "How did I end up in a reactive position and what do I need to do to move into a more proactive position?" Read and determine if what this book teaches is right for you. If it is, then take it step-by-step so you can move into a more proactive position.

SCORE: 29-31
JUST A FEW SLIGHT TWEAKS AWAY

You probably have a good grasp of the big picture. However, there still may be some uncertainty in how to handle certain situations. Maybe there are a few questions about a few of your investments and what you would do under certain rare but possible situations.

All investments have benefits and detriments. One of the best things you can do moving forward is to focus on the detriments of your investments so you can use the process and plan to put together your own personal protocol on what to do and when. The overall goal is to be able to keep income coming in, regardless of various conditions. This book can help you do that.

> ## SCORE: 32+
> ## POTENTIALLY MORE POWERFUL PROTOCOLS

You probably have thought about most situations and what you would do. You are probably not concerned about income alone. Perhaps you are more concerned about how to take income while paying less in taxes. Or, how to take income while effectively growing your legacy assets.

As you go through the process, pay attention to the additional strategies that can help you strengthen your efforts in your legacy planning, tax planning, and so on. The purpose of a plan is to provide clarity while allowing multiple strategies to take form and help support your overall goals.

POPULAR INCOME STRATEGY #5: THE RENTAL REAL ESTATE PORTFOLIO

Investment real estate is a different ball game altogether. The asset itself is unlike any of the more common investment options. Those who were fortunate enough to purchase investment real estate during their 20s and 30s most likely enjoyed a significant amount of tax advantages while their renters paid for the equity.

At some point, though, landlords get tired of being landlords. Whether it's the toilets, trash, or dealing with tenants, it's not uncommon for a landlord to want to retire from being a landlord.

There's a problem, though. Let's say you have a large portfolio in investment real estate, and you've depreciated the asset all the way. If you were to sell, the capital gains could take around 30% or more of the total value. That's a tough pill to swallow.

So, what do you do? Many will look for management companies to take care of everything, but that eats into cash flow. Also, there may be some repairs that are needed, but you've been putting them off for one reason or another. Maybe they are too high to rationalize any sort of return on investment. Either way, this is why many landlords feel stuck somewhere between a rock and a hard place.

For those who qualify as accredited investors, you may have a tax-efficient way out. You've probably heard of 1031 exchanges. If not, the quick definition is a 1031 exchange allows you to use the proceeds of the sale of an investment property to purchase another like-kind investment and not pay any capital gains tax.

"But Mike, why would I move my assets from one property to another when I want to be done with properties altogether?"

This is where the second part comes in. Have you heard of Delaware statutory trusts? They qualify as like-kind investments for 1031 exchanges. Essentially, they allow you to be a fractional owner of an investment property. You can maintain your cash flow without worrying about tenants, loans, or repairs.

This book does not dive deeper into 1031 exchanges or DSTs, but I want to mention it, so you know there are other options outside of selling everything, paying an arm and a leg in taxes, and then buying a bunch of other investments. Too often, I've heard of financial professionals advising their clients to just sell their properties. I believe it is because they might not know about these strategies.

If you have rental real estate, keep reading. Chances are, you have other assets that can help support the quality of life you want. As you go through the process, you will see places where your rental income or your DST income can play a role in your overall plan.

Like I said, I want to help you. This book is full of surprises and strategies you may not have known existed. So, keep reading.

Let's take a moment and do a quick Success Check-in Exercise. This is only for those who have investment real estate. If you do not have rentals, then skip the assessment and I'll see you in the next chapter.

SUCCESS CHECK-IN EXERCISE

Below, rate yourself on a scale from 0–5 on how accurate the statements are—0 means "not accurate at all," and 5 means "most accurate."

Once you've rated yourself for each statement, total up your scores and then use the Answer Key to determine your next steps.

Success Check-in Statement	Self-Rating
I do not anticipate many major repairs on any of my properties.	
My properties are in good neighborhoods, residentially or commercially, and tend to attract quality tenants.	
When I turn 70 years old, I can see myself finding joy in hiring contractors or taking care of the repairs myself.	
If I were to hire (or if I have already hired) a management company, the return-on-investment cash flow would still be able to support the lifestyle I want.	
My net monthly cash flow, based on current market value of the property, minus taxes, repairs, and all other expenses, is currently competitive.	
I am still enjoying the tax benefits of depreciating my properties each year.	
I do not have any loans or leverage based on the property that could compromise my retirement.	

WHAT YOUR SCORE REALLY MEANS

SCORE: 0-19
CONSIDER SELLING YOUR INVESTMENT REAL ESTATE

If your score brought you here, chances are you are holding on to your properties because you don't want to pay the large sum in taxes. Don't let yourself enter into a difficult situation between you and your properties. There are many ways to sell your properties and maintain your income without paying an arm and a leg in taxes. If this is you, consider taking the total net-of-loan value of your properties and go through the book. I want you to see what your income could potentially be without being beholden to your properties.

Once you finish the book, schedule a call with me or my team so we can discuss your exit strategies. These are investments that you can only access through a licensed financial professional. If I could point you in a self-sufficient direction that didn't require a professional, I would. Schedule a call by going to www.kedrec.com/call

SCORE: 20+
CONSIDER KEEPING YOUR INVESTMENT REAL ESTATE

It is important to have purpose in retirement. For many landlords, there seems to be a significant amount of joy going to Home Depot or Lowe's, getting the needed materials, and fixing normal wear and tear around the house. If your score brought you here, then chances are, you should keep your properties.

Keep reading the book and discover how you can incorporate your rental income stream and other assets in a coordinated effort to help maximize your income and quality of life.

Key Chapter Takeaways

- **4% Rule Takeaway:** The sequence of returns matters. Having too much at risk can put you in a difficult spot, especially if you were to experience a market crash early on in your retirement. Whatever you do, follow the Principle of Income and design your plan in such a way that you never have to pull income from an account that has experienced significant losses.

- **Annuitized Income Takeaway:** Inflation can erode your ability to afford the cost of the lifestyle you want. Deciding what your income is going to be now and potentially 20 to 30 years down the road could be considered a risky decision, especially when you consider the decision is irrevocable and your lifestyle needs could change at any moment.

- **Pension Income Takeaway:** Pensions are rare, yet wonderful options. Just make sure you are aware of the fund that supports the pension. Also, be prepared for whatever taxes may do in the future. If you want more control, that means you may have to take on more risk and responsibility, but that could mean more money to pass to your heirs.

- **Dividend Income Takeaway:** How much risk are you willing to take in order to get the dividend you need in order to sustain your desired quality of life? Dividend income strategies lack a reasonable backup plan. When markets go down, you may be forced to sell positions, which could compromise your retirement for years to come.

- **Rental Income Takeaway:** If you are a tired landlord, there are tax-efficient ways out. Though the book won't be discussing them in great detail, take comfort in knowing that the only way out is not selling it and potentially paying an arm and a leg in taxes.

Chapter 4

THE PRINCIPAL GUARANTEED RESERVOIR™

"Only when the tide goes out do you discover who's been swimming naked."

– Warren Buffet

You've got three markets to plan for: up markets, down markets, and flat markets. In up markets, you can pull income anywhere without much of a problem. Flat markets are really a combination of mostly up markets and a few really bad down markets. Ultimately, the problem we are trying to solve is how to pull income from your accounts when markets go down without accentuating your losses while also maintaining enough flexibility to adjust your plan and income along the way.

The Principle of Income suggests that you should never draw income from an account that has experienced significant losses. Failing to do so may have negative effects on your income and assets and may ultimately compromise your retirement. Remember earlier in the book when I took you through the exercise of what would happen if your account went down by -30%? As a quick reminder, a -30% loss would take a 43% return just to break even. Now, assume you took 4% from your portfolio when you had already lost -30%. At that point, you would be down -34% overall, which would require a 50% return just to break even.

When you follow the Principle of Income, you address a major potential problem in retirement, sequence of returns risk. Basically, if you can avoid taking income from accounts that have lost money, you do yourself and your investments a huge favor. The problem is we don't know when the markets are going to crash. No one knows the future.

This is where the Principal Guaranteed Reservoir™ comes in. Imagine allocating a portion of your assets into investments or products that cannot lose any principal (money). When markets go down, you draw income from your reservoir. That's it. It is so simple, yet so important I'm going to say it again.

When markets are up, you can take income anywhere.

When markets go down, you pull income from your Principal Guaranteed Reservoir™.

By not accentuating your losses, you allow your accounts the potential to recover faster. By not accentuating your losses, you are protecting your cash value return on investment (remember the 6% vs. 8% return comparison). The Principal Guaranteed Reservoir™ helps you not dig holes so deep you can't climb out of them.

I cannot emphasize enough what a game changer it is to be able to support a plan designed to never require you to take income from accounts that have experienced significant losses. You don't need to be a sophisticated investor who perfectly times the market. You just need to make sure your reservoir is full and liquid enough to keep your income coming in should things get ugly in the market.

You fill up your reservoir, based on what your plan would suggest. As you enjoy your retirement, you slowly and deliberately drain your reservoir. When you retire, you will probably need a bigger reservoir than when you are 10 to 15 years in. When implemented correctly, this simple strategy helps solve sequence of returns risk, the risk that makes the 4% Rule potentially risky.

The Principal Guaranteed Reservoir™ also allows you to be flexible in your plan and portfolio while maintaining an appropriate amount of protection from down markets. You could argue that the Principal Guaranteed Reservoir™ strategy makes the annuitized income stream obsolete.

To keep going, you would have potentially less risk than your standard market-based portfolio, opening the door to consider the lump sum option. That would give you more control over your income and how you could prepare it to be passed to your heirs. Lastly, you can invest with more confidence in the market, putting yourself in charge of the "dividends" you want from your portfolio.

This strategy cannot be accomplished by any one carrier, custodian, or company. There is no single product that you can buy to make it all work. It is a self-sustaining financial ecosystem. Each investment or product plays a role in the overall portfolio.

Now, you might have some questions. Let's get to some answers about the Principal Guaranteed Reservoir™.

Question #1: What Investments or Products Qualify For the Principal Guaranteed Reservoir™?

All investments can offer you reasonable growth potential, principal protection, and liquidity. The problem is *each investment can only offer you two of the three characteristics.* Here's a simple graphic to illustrate my point.

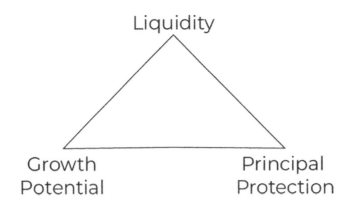

In the example below, principal protection and liquidity would characterize checking, savings, and money market accounts. At the risk of being redundant, you can't have liquidity, principal protection, *and* reasonable growth potential.

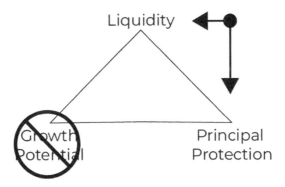

Growth potential with reasonable liquidity would characterize your stocks, mutual funds, and ETFs. It may take a couple of days to settle before you get your funds, but they are pretty liquid.

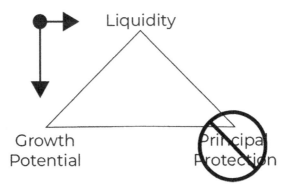

Both groups don't work for the reservoir. One lacks sufficient growth potential, which you need to be able to keep up with inflation. The other lacks sufficient protection, which you also need for this strategy to work.

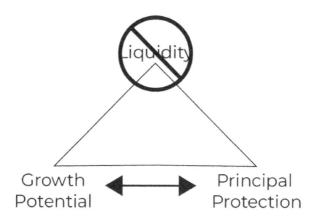

The Principal Guaranteed Reservoir™ needs investments or products that offer reasonable growth potential to help keep up with inflation and principal protection so that when markets go down, they don't lose money. There are only four financial products that I believe qualify. They are:

- U.S. Treasuries, if held to maturity
- Certificates of Deposit
- Fixed or Fixed-Indexed annuities, if not annuitized
- Cash value life insurance

Each of these options has its own benefits and detriments. At this point, it is too early to tell which ones make sense because we have not made your plan, yet. Remember, you need a plan in place before you can discuss strategies.

Question #2: How much do I need to put into a Principal Guaranteed Reservoir™ for this to work?

It's too early to tell. It will all depend on your plan. For those who want to front load your plan and travel, there's a good chance you might lean heavier on U.S. Treasuries as you fund your reservoir. For those who are planning to retire in three to five years or so, you may consider a combination of CDs and annuities. For those who have assets they won't need for ten years, and they are anticipating a higher than desirable taxable situation, and are healthy, you may end up considering cash value life insurance. If you go down that path, please make sure you are in need of the death benefit you'll be paying for as well as the fees involved with the product. I'll explain more later.

Overall, it's too early to tell how much should go into your reservoir. But, I want to get the options out in the open so you can keep them in the back of your mind as you go through Part 2.

Question #3: Is it possible that I don't need a Principal Guaranteed Reservoir™?

Yes. If you are getting the income you need and want from income sources, such as rental income, DST income, pension income, and so on, then your assets would in theory be focused on building a legacy to pass. You probably only need the reservoir if you plan on taking income from your assets that are not already providing you with an income stream.

The purpose of the Principal Guaranteed Reservoir™ is to keep income coming in from your portfolio without accentuating losses in the down year. Everyone's plan is different. Therefore, how much you put into the reservoir, if anything at all, is entirely dependent on you and your plan.

The proper sequence is to build the plan first and then let the plan and principles help guide the implementation of the strategies, like the Principal Guaranteed Reservoir™.

In Part 2, we will build the plan, run the calculations and scenarios that will help guide what should go into your Principal Guaranteed Reservoir™, and decide how to structure it so liquidity is not a significant issue. **If you aren't yet absolutely clear on how a Principal Guaranteed Reservoir™ works, that's okay. We're going to be talking about it a lot in the coming chapters.**

We've got one more chapter before Part 2. Though it is short, it is still very important.

I'll see you there.

Key Chapter Takeaways

- When markets go up, you can take income anywhere. When markets go down, you take income from your Principal Guaranteed Reservoir™.

- Investments and products that qualify for the Principal Guaranteed Reservoir™ include U.S. Treasuries, if held to maturity, CDs, Fixed or Fixed-Indexed annuities, and cash value life insurance, like indexed universal life insurance.

- You cannot know how much should go into the Principal Guaranteed Reservoir™, if any at all, until you put your plan together. Plan before you talk about strategies, investments, and products.

Chapter 5

PROTECTION HAS A PRICE

"A man [or woman] cannot have his cake and eat his cake."

— Thomas, Duke of Norfolk

Years ago, a friend told me an interesting story about a client who came in with a specific request. The well-intended client expressed frustration with the market. He said, "Is there an investment that offers significant growth potential, next-day liquidity, principal protection, and guaranteed income for life?"

My friend responded, "Do you want it to have tax advantages too?"

The client said, "Yes! That'd be great!"

My friend smiled. "I wish that were possible, but that doesn't exist."

There is no such thing as a perfect investment.

For the Principal Guaranteed Reservoir™ strategy to work, you must have a reservoir of assets that have principal protection so you can draw income without accentuating losses. That means you are funding assets that either offer liquidity and principal protection, like your savings account, or you are funding assets that offer reasonable growth potential and principal protection, like CDs.

Giving up some liquidity is, in many people's minds, a big ask. It's often new and can feel uncomfortable. As previously stated, no investment can offer you everything you could want or need.

We believe it is mission critical to have a way to protect at least a portion of your assets when the market goes down or stays flat. Remember, bonds are not considered principal guaranteed if you end up selling them before they mature. Also, they are only as good as the issuer.

Relying on your ability to get every trade right is statistically improbable. I would argue having a reasonable portion of your assets protected may be one of the most important characteristics of your portfolio. But, it comes at a price.

Protection requires patience and discipline.

Do you need 100% access to all of your funds in retirement at any given time? Probably not. The only situation I can think of is the need to spend everything you have for a life-saving emergency. If that were to happen, then you wouldn't have anything left in retirement, which would be a problem unto itself.

What you likely need is access to some funds now and access to some funds later. There's a good chance you'll need income for at least twenty years, if not longer. This is where patience and discipline come in.

Let me explain with a few examples. Arguably, I think that one of the "best" features of a qualified account (like your 401(k) or IRA) is the fact that if you take income out too early, you get hit with a 10% early withdrawal penalty. That helps people keep their retirement savings in those accounts, so they have it when they retire.

The same could be said about investments and products that qualify for the Principal Guaranteed Reservoir™ (e.g., Treasuries, CDs, fixed annuities, fixed-index annuities, and cash value life insurance policies). No one likes giving up liquidity. But is it worth it to know that a portion of your portfolio can't lose money when markets crash? I would argue yes. Does it help you stay disciplined in your retirement spending so that you can potentially have income now and have income later? I would argue yes as well.

Every decision we make in life is nothing more than a trade. We give up something to gain something. When we get married, we give up being single and available to anyone to being intimately available and dedicated to an individual person while hoping the "trade" is beneficial for all parties involved.

When we have kids, we give up many freedoms, including a good night's sleep, and hope that in the end, the experience will be worth it. Most parents say having kids was the best thing they ever did. Was it hard? Yes. Did it require patience and discipline? Yes.

The trade we must make to protect ourselves from down markets is by using various financial vehicles that may require us to give up full liquidity for a period of time. There's no way around it.

If you can't live with the idea of having any part of your portfolio lacking liquidity for a certain amount of time, then you may want to save yourself some time and stop reading this book. We are going to discuss a series of strategies that can work together for your benefit. Everything in life is a trade. You've got to give something in order to gain something in return. Many people are looking for the perfect investment. It just doesn't exist.

If you are looking for that perfect investment, there's nothing I can do or say to help you. In addition, and based on my research, I cannot endorse the idea of keeping all of your assets at risk. Markets have a history of crashing every 7–8 years. In my opinion, it's only a matter of time until you will be forced to accentuate your losses by drawing income during a market crash. I wish you the best.

For the rest of us who are willing to accept the fact that by giving up some liquidity in our portfolio we will be more prepared to keep our income coming in without having to accentuate losses when the market crashes. I look forward to seeing you in the next chapter.

Key Chapter Takeaways

- There is no such thing as a perfect investment.

- Protection requires patience and discipline.

- Every decision we make in life is a trade. Often, we need to give up something in order to gain what we desire.

Part 2

THE FUNCTIONAL
WEALTH PLAN™

Chapter 6

PLAN FOR THE GAP

"Dare to live the life you have dreamed for yourself. Go forward and make your dreams come true."

– Ralph Waldo Emerson

It's time to start building your plan. At the end of the chapter, I'll give you a link and some homework. Before we start the planning process, **I want to introduce you to the Principle of Planning, which suggests that predetermined guidelines can help increase your probability of future success**. Failing to set proper guidelines can cause you to make reactive and possibly emotional decisions that could eventually compromise your retirement.

We know that the markets will either go up, go down, or stay flat next year. We know that taxes, inflation, and other factors will continue to evolve over time. We can't do anything about it. But we can create a plan that puts us in a proactive position that can help increase our probability of success overall. The first step when it comes to putting a preliminary plan together is to plan for the gap.

To start, you'll need to understand the order in which your retirement plan must be organized. Each adjustment you make within your plan will have a rippling effect on your overall income and projected net worth. In most situations, the objective is to either maximize your income or maximize your estate in a tax-efficient manner so that your beneficiaries get as much as possible. Either way, even the most subtle adjustments can have significant effects on your plan.

The best way I know how to explain this process is with a simple analogy. Let's say you have a jar that must be filled. All you have to work with is a pile of small rocks and a pile of sand. Your job is to get all of the rocks and sand into the jar.

If you put the sand in first and then all the rocks, the rocks won't fit. The rocks will sit on top of the sand. However, if you put the rocks in first and then the sand, the sand will slowly fill all of the gaps and crevices, filling up 100% of the jar.

Social Security, Pensions, Rental Income, and Other Income Streams

Income Generated From Your Portfolio

When it comes to retirement, you must first fill your "retirement jar" with your "rocks." In other words, line up the different expected income streams based on when you plan to start receiving income. Examples include your Social Security benefit, pension(s), rental real estate income, and so on. Once they are all lined up, the sand represents your portfolio income. Our software will help you fill in all the gaps and crevices so that your retirement income is smooth, year over year with a cost-of-living adjustment to help offset inflation.

Make sure you have the following information readily available:

- The year you want to retire
- The annual net of tax income you want when you retire
- The annual amount in Social Security benefits expected at full retirement age for yourself (and for your spouse if married)
- Total amount of investable assets
- Your effective tax rate
- Pension start date and survivability options, if applicable
- Rental cash flow information, if applicable
- An understanding of family longevity and life expectancy

There may be additional information needed based on your unique situation. Please take a moment and consider anything else that may affect your financial situation.

Now that you've got all your ducks in a row, are you ready to get started?

THE HYPOTHETICAL EXAMPLE

When you start creating a Functional Wealth Plan™, it can feel overwhelming. There is no simple way to do it. Let's run through quickly what the results could look like. Here is a hypothetical example of the math behind a Functional Wealth Plan™. I'll explain in greater detail further in this chapter how to come up with the numbers to populate this tool, but here's a glance at what the end result might look like:

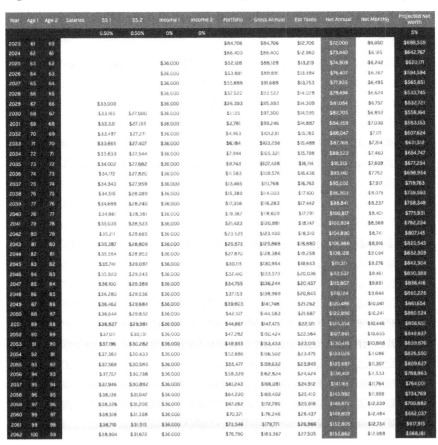

Year	Age 1	Age 2	Salaries	SS 1	SS 2	Income 1	Income 2	Portfolio	Gross Annual	Est Taxes	Net Annual	Net Monthly	Projected Net Worth
				0.50%	0.50%	0%	0%						5%
2023	61	60							$84,706	$84,706	$12,706	$72,000	$6,000	$698,559
2024	62	61							$86,400	$86,400	$12,960	$73,440	$6,120	$642,767
2025	63	62				$36,000		$52,128	$88,128	$13,219	$74,909	$6,242	$620,171
2026	64	63				$36,000		$53,691	$89,691	$13,484	$76,407	$6,367	$584,594
2027	65	64				$36,000		$55,688	$91,688	$13,753	$77,935	$6,495	$565,851
2028	66	65				$36,000		$57,522	$93,522	$14,028	$79,494	$6,624	$533,745
2029	67	66	$33,000			$36,000		$26,393	$95,393	$14,309	$81,084	$6,757	$532,721
2030	68	67	$33,165	$27,000		$36,000		$1,135	$97,300	$14,595	$82,705	$6,892	$558,164
2031	68	68	$33,331	$27,135		$36,000		$2,781	$99,246	$14,887	$84,359	$7,030	$583,153
2032	70	69	$33,497	$27,271		$36,000		$4,463	$101,231	$15,185	$86,047	$7,171	$607,624
2033	71	70	$33,665	$27,407		$36,000		$6,184	$103,256	$15,488	$87,768	$7,314	$631,512
2034	72	71	$33,833	$27,544		$36,000		$7,944	$105,321	$15,798	$89,523	$7,460	$654,747
2035	73	72	$34,002	$27,682		$36,000		$9,743	$107,428	$16,114	$91,313	$7,609	$677,294
2036	74	73	$34,172	$27,820		$36,000		$11,583	$109,576	$16,436	$93,140	$7,762	$698,954
2037	75	74	$34,343	$27,959		$36,000		$13,465	$111,768	$16,765	$95,002	$7,917	$719,763
2038	76	75	$34,515	$28,099		$36,000		$15,389	$114,003	$17,100	$86,803	$8,075	$739,593
2039	77	76	$34,688	$28,240		$36,000		$17,356	$116,283	$17,442	$88,841	$8,237	$758,349
2040	78	77	$34,861	$28,381		$36,000		$19,367	$118,609	$17,791	$100,817	$8,401	$775,931
2041	79	78	$35,035	$28,523		$36,000		$21,423	$120,981	$18,147	$102,834	$8,569	$792,234
2042	80	79	$35,211	$28,665		$36,000		$23,525	$123,400	$18,510	$104,890	$8,741	$807,145
2043	81	80	$35,387	$28,809		$36,000		$25,673	$125,868	$18,880	$106,988	$8,916	$820,545
2044	82	81	$35,564	$28,953		$36,000		$27,870	$128,386	$19,258	$109,128	$9,094	$832,309
2045	83	82	$35,741	$29,097		$36,000		$30,115	$130,954	$19,643	$111,311	$9,276	$842,304
2046	84	83	$35,920	$29,243		$36,000		$32,410	$133,573	$20,036	$113,537	$9,461	$850,389
2047	85	84	$36,100	$29,389		$36,000		$34,755	$136,244	$20,437	$115,807	$9,651	$856,416
2048	86	85	$36,280	$29,536		$36,000		$37,153	$138,969	$20,845	$118,124	$9,844	$860,226
2049	87	86	$36,462	$29,684		$36,000		$39,603	$141,748	$21,262	$120,486	$10,041	$861,654
2050	88	87	$36,644	$29,832		$36,000		$42,107	$144,583	$21,687	$122,896	$10,241	$860,524
2051	89	88	$36,827	$29,981		$36,000		$44,667	$147,475	$22,121	$125,354	$10,446	$856,651
2052	90	89	$37,011	$30,131		$36,000		$47,282	$150,424	$22,564	$127,861	$10,655	$849,837
2053	91	90	$37,196	$30,282		$36,000		$49,955	$153,433	$23,015	$130,418	$10,868	$839,876
2054	92	91	$37,382	$30,433		$36,000		$52,686	$156,502	$23,475	$133,026	$11,086	$826,550
2055	93	92	$37,569	$30,585		$36,000		$55,477	$159,632	$23,945	$135,687	$11,307	$809,627
2056	94	93	$37,757	$30,738		$36,000		$58,329	$162,824	$24,424	$138,401	$11,533	$788,863
2057	95	94	$37,946	$30,892		$36,000		$61,243	$166,081	$24,912	$141,169	$11,764	$764,001
2058	96	95	$38,136	$31,047		$36,000		$64,220	$169,402	$25,410	$143,992	$11,999	$734,769
2059	97	96	$38,326	$31,202		$36,000		$67,262	$172,790	$25,919	$146,872	$12,239	$700,882
2060	98	97	$38,518	$31,358		$36,000		$70,371	$176,246	$26,437	$149,809	$12,484	$662,037
2061	99	98	$38,710	$31,515		$36,000		$73,546	$179,771	$26,966	$152,806	$12,734	$617,915
2062	100	99	$38,904	$31,672		$36,000		$76,790	$183,367	$27,505	$155,862	$12,988	$568,181

Hypothetical illustration shown for demonstration purposes only. It is not guaranteed and not indicative of your actual plan results.

Looks like a lot, right? Let me break it down step by step starting with the top left.

By the way, the plan we are about to go through was created with the software that you'll be able to use when you finish the book. It is one of the many bonuses I have included. Please read to the end of the book, though, so you have context and use this tool correctly. Let's keep going.

The first column shows the years. This plan starts in 2023 and continues until 2062.

The second and third columns are the ages of the couple. Based on their family history, they expect to live to their late 80s but wanted to plan until age 100, just in case.

The next column shows current employment income. For our example, this couple is retiring this year, so I left the salary information blank.

Moving on to the right, you'll notice two columns named SS 1 and SS 2. You guessed it, that stands for Social Security 1, as in the Social Security benefit for spouse number 1 and Social Security 2 for spouse number 2.

Next, you will see Income 1, which is a pension. The couple has not elected to take the pension, yet. At this moment, they want to compare their options.

The column labeled "Portfolio" represents the income generated from the portfolio, or in other words, your investable assets, like stocks, mutual funds, CDs, and so on.

Notice how the portfolio amounts each year go up and down. Remember, this is the sand from our earlier analogy. It is designed to bridge the gap between the rocks (in this case, the pension and Social Security benefits) so that you can enjoy a smooth income in retirement.

In 2025, you'll see the portfolio income amount went down from $86,400 to $52,128. This is because in that same year, they would turn on their pension and start receiving $36,000 per year. That means the portfolio will need to provide less income, hence why it went down.

Notice how the same thing happens when Social Security starts. Sometimes, you'll notice the Portfolio goes negative. That means your income streams are producing more than what the target net annual income needs. You can either enjoy the raise and adjust your plan, or invest the excess.

Next, we have Gross Income, Estimated Taxes, and Net Income. The idea with these three columns is to first focus on your net income since that is what you are expected to actually get and be able to spend. Let's start with the net income column.

This couple wanted $6,000 a month, net of tax (after income tax and capital gains taxes were paid). They wanted a relatively simple retirement with very little travel. All of their kids and grandkids lived nearby, which made things convenient. In reality, they only needed around $4,000 per month to live comfortably, based on their desired lifestyle. The additional money is intended to be for random events, trips, and so on.

Please note, that this is just one hypothetical couple's account. I've seen people want to retire with less. I've built plans that gave the couple over $20,000 in income per month. It all depends on what you have and what you want. Okay, now back to the net income column.

Notice how the net income column consistently increases by 2% each year? That's the cost-of-living adjustment (COLA). Some people will want to illustrate a higher COLA while others might want a lower COLA. It all depends on your unique situations and expectations.

As a general rule, there are two phases in retirement. You've got your travel years and your casual years. Your first ten years are typically your travel years. This is typically when you will be the most active. You may want to spend more during those years than in your casual years, and that's okay.

My only word of caution is not to have too much fun at the beginning of retirement. With health care costs on the rise, you don't want to spend so much that you can't afford to support yourself later on. That is why having a healthy cost-of-living adjustment is so important. We'll talk about strategies to frontload a plan later.

Next, let's look at the estimated taxes column. We don't know what future tax brackets will be. We can't anticipate future tax laws that could reshape retirement accounts. Estimated Taxes is a column that offers our best guess projections based on the current tax environment.

Now that we've discussed the net income column and the estimated tax column, let's finish this up with the gross income column. As you can imagine, this column estimates how much gross (pre-tax) income is needed to get the net income you want.

The last column shows the projected net worth. This column represents all of your investable assets, not including your primary residence. It grows at an assumed 5% annual rate. Why 5%? Just like there are over-the-counter drugs and prescription drugs, I set it at 5% so that you could not over-promise yourself future projections. Greed is a powerful emotion, and I want to help bridle it.

What if you get more than 5% returns for several years? Rerun your plan and enjoy the extra funds. I believe it is better to be conservative with a pleasant surprise than to try and overdo it and have to go back to work in your 70s and 80s.

In the next chapter, once your plan is built, we will talk about strategies, market patterns, and more. Then you can better understand the potential problems you may face and your options to address them.

One of the most common questions I get is, "Should I protect my net worth and only live off of the gains, or can I spend it down?" Like most other answers I've given, it depends.

It depends on your risk tolerance. Are you okay with the thought of spending it down? It depends on your estate and legacy planning. Do you want to leave a significant inheritance to your kids or beneficiaries? Some do and some don't.

Many people want to maximize their income and leave as little as possible to their kids. There is nothing wrong with that mindset. It all depends on what you want.

If you want a recommendation to help you get started, try to adjust your income so that the projected net worth on the year you retire is roughly the same as your life expectancy. That can help you measure how to preserve principal while letting it go down a little after your life expectancy date. Regardless of how things project, just make sure that your projections do not go negative. Take a look at the bottom right of the plan. If those numbers are negative, that means you probably cannot afford to retire and receive the income you are projecting.

Now that we have discussed how to put together your preliminary Functional Wealth Plan™, it's time to talk about how to optimize income streams. Since Social Security optimization is the most common request I get, we can start there.

If you've stayed with me up to this point, we've covered a lot in a very short amount of time. If you need anything clarified, if you have questions, or if there's something else, I want to offer my team's support, should you need it.

Please visit www.kedrec.com/call and schedule a 30-minute chat.

We offer multiple services to help you accomplish every single step listed in the book and more.

SOCIAL SECURITY OPTIMIZATION

Your Social Security can help you increase your overall income or help you protect your estate from dwindling down too fast, but usually not both. Here's another way of saying it.

"If you file too early, your income could be hurting.
But if you file too late, you could be hurting your estate."

Let's assume, for example, that you retire at 60 years old. Congratulations, you are now enjoying some of the best years of your life. If you were to wait and file for Social Security at 70 years old, you would need to pull additional income from assets between 60 and 70 years old to bridge the gap.

When you turned 70, you would receive your maximum benefit. You would also be able to lower the amount of income needed from your portfolio when you file for your Social Security benefit. Sounds nice until you realize the cost. "If you filed too late, you may be hurting your estate." That ten-year gap between when you retire at 60 years old and when you file for Social Security at age 70 likely requires you to reduce your portfolio (estate) in order to make it work.

If you were to file at 62 years old, then you would be filing for Social Security at a "discount". Even though you would not need to pull as much income from your portfolio, it can have an overall negative effect on the maximum income you could receive in retirement. Since you have taken an income reduction that lasts a lifetime, you'll feel it for the rest of your life. Therefore, "If you file too early, your income may be hurting."

The easiest way to tell which option is best for you is to run the numbers. On your Social Security benefits statement, you should have estimated monthly benefits amounts for every year between 62 and 70 years old. First, let's enter the numbers into the software and see what happens if both spouses were to file at 62 years old. Remember to adjust the monthly benefit amount and the age. Here's what it would look like.

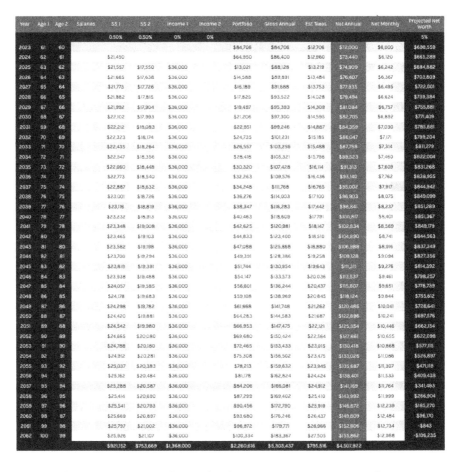

Hypothetical illustration shown for demonstration purposes only. It is not guaranteed and not indicative of your actual plan results.

Notice how the left column maintains a higher projected net worth balance for most of the plan. Because there is very little income needed from the portfolio, the portfolio has more growth potential. The total projected net worth doesn't start to dip until the early 80s. If you were to pass before the age of 80, filing for an early benefit could lead to additional funds passed to your heirs.

Now, let's rerun the plan, only this time, you're filing at age 70. Here's what it should look like.

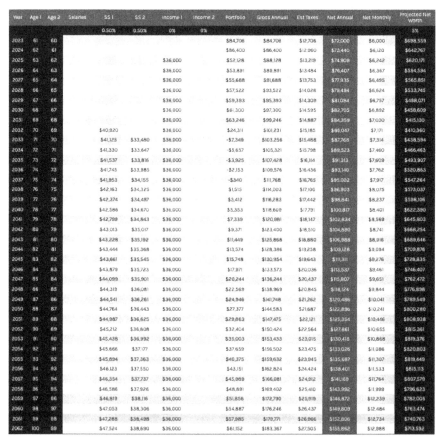

Year	Age 1	Age 2	Salaries	SS 1	SS 2	Income 1	Income 2	Portfolio	Gross Annual	Est Taxes	Net Annual	Net Monthly	Projected Net Worth
				0.50%	0.50%	0%	0%						5%
2023	61	60						$84,706	$84,706	$12,706	$72,000	$6,000	$698,559
2024	62	61						$86,400	$86,400	$12,960	$73,440	$6,120	$642,767
2025	63	62					$36,000	$52,128	$88,128	$13,219	$74,909	$6,242	$620,171
2026	64	63					$36,000	$53,891	$89,891	$13,484	$76,407	$6,367	$584,584
2027	65	64					$36,000	$55,688	$91,688	$13,753	$77,935	$6,495	$565,851
2028	66	65					$36,000	$57,522	$93,522	$14,028	$78,494	$6,624	$533,745
2029	67	66					$36,000	$59,393	$95,393	$14,309	$81,084	$6,757	$498,071
2030	68	67					$36,000	$61,300	$97,300	$14,595	$82,705	$6,892	$458,609
2031	69	68					$36,000	$63,246	$99,246	$14,887	$84,359	$7,030	$415,130
2032	70	69	$40,920				$36,000	$24,311	$101,231	$15,185	$86,047	$7,171	$410,360
2033	71	70	$41,125	$33,480			$36,000	-$7,349	$103,256	$15,488	$87,768	$7,314	$438,584
2034	72	71	$41,330	$33,647			$36,000	-$5,657	$105,321	$15,798	$89,523	$7,460	$466,463
2035	73	72	$41,537	$33,816			$36,000	-$3,925	$107,428	$16,114	$91,313	$7,609	$483,907
2036	74	73	$41,745	$33,985			$36,000	-$2,153	$109,576	$16,436	$93,140	$7,762	$520,863
2037	75	74	$41,953	$34,155			$36,000	-$340	$111,768	$16,765	$95,002	$7,917	$547,264
2038	76	75	$42,163	$34,325			$36,000	$1,515	$114,003	$17,100	$96,803	$8,075	$573,037
2039	77	76	$42,374	$34,497			$36,000	$3,412	$116,283	$17,442	$98,841	$8,237	$598,106
2040	78	77	$42,586	$34,670			$36,000	$5,353	$118,609	$17,791	$100,817	$8,401	$622,390
2041	79	78	$42,799	$34,843			$36,000	$7,339	$120,981	$18,147	$102,834	$8,569	$645,803
2042	80	79	$43,013	$35,017			$36,000	$9,371	$123,400	$18,510	$104,890	$8,741	$668,254
2043	81	80	$43,228	$35,192			$36,000	$11,449	$125,868	$18,880	$106,988	$8,916	$689,646
2044	82	81	$43,444	$35,368			$36,000	$13,574	$128,386	$19,258	$109,128	$9,094	$709,876
2045	83	82	$43,661	$35,545			$36,000	$15,748	$130,954	$19,643	$111,311	$9,276	$728,835
2046	84	83	$43,879	$35,723			$36,000	$17,971	$133,573	$20,036	$113,537	$9,461	$746,407
2047	85	84	$44,099	$35,901			$36,000	$20,244	$136,244	$20,437	$115,807	$9,651	$762,472
2048	86	85	$44,319	$36,081			$36,000	$22,569	$138,969	$20,845	$118,124	$9,844	$776,898
2049	87	86	$44,541	$36,261			$36,000	$24,946	$141,748	$21,262	$120,486	$10,041	$789,549
2050	88	87	$44,764	$36,443			$36,000	$27,377	$144,583	$21,687	$122,896	$10,241	$800,280
2051	89	88	$44,987	$36,625			$36,000	$29,863	$147,475	$22,121	$125,354	$10,446	$808,938
2052	90	89	$45,212	$36,808			$36,000	$32,404	$150,424	$22,564	$127,861	$10,655	$815,361
2053	91	90	$45,438	$36,992			$36,000	$35,003	$153,433	$23,015	$130,418	$10,868	$819,376
2054	92	91	$45,666	$37,177			$36,000	$37,659	$156,502	$23,475	$133,026	$11,086	$820,803
2055	93	92	$45,894	$37,363			$36,000	$40,375	$159,632	$23,945	$135,687	$11,307	$819,449
2056	94	93	$46,123	$37,550			$36,000	$43,151	$162,824	$24,424	$138,401	$11,533	$815,113
2057	95	94	$46,354	$37,737			$36,000	$45,989	$166,081	$24,912	$141,169	$11,764	$807,579
2058	96	95	$46,586	$37,926			$36,000	$48,891	$169,402	$25,410	$143,992	$11,999	$796,623
2059	97	96	$46,819	$38,116			$36,000	$51,856	$172,790	$25,919	$146,872	$12,239	$782,005
2060	98	97	$47,053	$38,306			$36,000	$54,887	$176,246	$26,437	$149,809	$12,484	$763,474
2061	99	98	$47,288	$38,498			$36,000	$57,985	$179,771	$26,966	$152,806	$12,734	$740,763
2062	100	99	$47,524	$38,690			$36,000	$61,152	$183,367	$27,505	$155,862	$12,988	$713,592

Hypothetical illustration shown for demonstration purposes only. It is not guaranteed and not indicative of your actual plan results.

Notice how the projected net worth goes down significantly over the first 10 years of the plan. Once Social Security starts, the overall portfolio then begins to recover. What's important here is the responsibility of the portfolio income column. Notice how it is doing some heavy lifting and providing most of the retirement income until the year 2032.

Those years will be the make-or-break years of this retirement plan. If the markets were to crash and they pulled that much income from their portfolio, it could be devastating. For the first two years, the plan is suggesting pulling over 10% of their income! We'll talk more about this later, but in this version, having a Principal Guaranteed Reservoir™ liquid enough to keep income coming in during those first ten years will be incredibly important.

However, notice how once Social Security starts, the portfolio income goes negative. That means there's more income coming in from the income streams than is needed. From that point on, the portfolio becomes a complement to the overall income strategy instead of shouldering the responsibility of providing the majority of the needed income.

For those who have saved less than $250,000 for retirement, I want to be upfront about the strategy you should consider. If you have saved $250,000 in assets or less for retirement, there is a good chance that Social Security will be your main source of retirement income.

If that is true, then let me suggest what you may want to do...

Consider working as long as you can, or until age 70. When you cannot work any longer, retire and file for Social Security.

If you are able to work past 70 years old, file for Social Security at that point and keep working as long as you want.

By waiting until 70 or when you retire to file for Social Security, you will not have to pull as much income from your assets, helping preserve your assets while they continue to grow as much as possible. If you plan to work past 70 years old, I suggest you still take your benefits at 70 years old. It won't grow past your 70th birthday.

Pension Income vs. Lump Sum

Let's talk about your pension. At some point, you will need to decide between taking the pension as income (lifetime payments) vs. taking the lump sum (one-time payment that is often rolled over into your Traditional IRA to be managed.)

If you take the lump sum, then they will ask you where it should be sent. Have it rolled over to a retirement plan such as an IRA. From that point on, it will be your responsibility to be a good steward over those assets and make them last longer than you. You, or your advisor, will need to effectively grow those assets while proactively minimizing the tax burdens.

Where there's more responsibility, there's also more opportunity. If you're comfortable with managing your own investments, or having a professional manage them for you, and would prefer to minimize your taxes now under the current tax environment (as opposed to waiting and seeing what happens in the future), then the lump sum option may be better for you. Ultimately, it gives you more control over the future tax situation.

Lastly, if you consider your projected net worth, especially during years one through ten of your retirement, a lump sum can be great for your beneficiaries should you and your spouse pass.

Don't pick the lump sum for your beneficiaries though. You need to pick what is best for you.

If you want less risk, consider taking the pension income. Even though you'll be taxed on it for life and it all goes away when you pass (and when your spouse passes, if applicable), there's comfort in a check showing up every month, regardless of the market. There's no shame in the pension option.

When you're ready to compare the lump sum vs. your pension income stream, the easiest way to see how it affects your retirement is to first put in the pension and run the numbers.

Notice the projected net worth amount at age 100. It is similar to the exercise you did with Social Security. You'll look at age 100 because you want to make sure that your retirement is projected to last longer than you.

Also, make sure to look at your projected net worth during the first ten years. I want you to be able to compare the pension income stream and the lump sum difference should you pass sooner than expected.

Next, take out the pension income and put in the lump sum dollar amount in your total net worth amount. Now, rerun the numbers without changing anything else. Look at your projected net worth in ten years and at age 100. Notice the difference and ask yourself which option you're more comfortable with.

For some employment plans, you can also take half of your lump sum and receive half of your pension for life. Try those numbers as well and see how they look. At the end of the day, there is no perfect solution here. It is based on your preferences and comfort level.

Real Estate and the Landlord's Exit Strategy

Let's talk about your rental portfolio. If you don't have any rental properties, you can skip this section by going to "Wrapping Up Your First Draft."

If you have rental income, the first thing you need to calculate is your return on investment. That number is based on the current home value and the net of taxes and expenses cash flow. Too often, landlords tell me what they make in rent and leave out the costs of repairs and taxes. That's an incomplete calculation.

now your net-of-expense return on investment, based on current market value, then you can have an apples-to-apples conversation. If your rental real estate is making less than the riskless rate, which is something the Fed determines, then it may be time to sell. If you are tired of dealing with tenants, toilets, roofs, and HVAC systems, then it may be time to retire from being a landlord. If that is you, consider reaching out to me and my team so we can have a conversation about 1031 exchanges and Delaware statutory trusts.

Just go to www.kedrec.com/call.

Do not put your properties up for sale until we talk. If they are already up for sale, schedule the call ASAP. There are many tight timelines around 1031 exchanges and exit strategies, based on IRS rules, that must be met. Best practice is to have the conversation first. Then put an exit plan together before the properties go up for sale. If you already sold your property or properties, it is probably too late.

If you are receiving more than the riskless rate, then it is up to you whether or not you want to keep it, sell it and pay the taxes, or do a 1031 exchange and defer the capital gains tax while maintaining cash flow.

If you want to keep the rental income, add the net-of-expenses monthly income to your plan in the same place that you would add a pension. If you increase rent every year, then make sure to consider adding a cost-of-living adjustment to your income stream. Plans depend on reasonable projections. Whatever you put in your plan must be implemented in real life. So, make sure you follow what you project in your plan.

Wrapping Up Your First Draft

Once you have created your plan, you should be able to answer the following questions:

- When can I retire?
- How much income should I expect in retirement?

- Can I afford to retire?
- When should I file for Social Security?
- Should I take the pension or the lump sum?
- What would my retirement look like when a spouse passes?
- And more

Now that we have the preliminary plan together, we can plan for the gaps and start designing the portfolio that can support the plan.

As a quick side note, at the end of the book in the bonus section, I'll give you links and resources to these tools and more so you can create your plan on your own. However, don't skip ahead and go right to the links. I want to make sure you see the entire process, from start to finish, so when it's your turn to create a plan and implement everything we are discussing, you will be able to put your plan together with the end in mind.

Take a breath.

You're doing great.

Let's bring this plan to life.

I'll see you in the next chapter.

P.S. If you are feeling slightly overwhelmed, remember we are here to help. You can always schedule a call with my team. Their job is to help you create a plan that's designed to last longer than you™. Just go to www.kedrec.com/call to schedule a quick call so you can learn more.

Chapter 7

SELECTING YOUR STRATEGIES

"Retirement is a blank sheet of paper. It is a chance to redesign your life into something new and different."

– Patrick Foley

Now that we have a plan, we can start to deliberately pick which investments and products should be in the portfolio. Before we discuss the options, I want to briefly review what we are trying to solve. Let's take a look at some of the historical market patterns you need to know.

First, since the 1950s, the S&P 500® has experienced around 38 market corrections. In other words, on average, every 1.8 years there have been market declines of 10% or worse since 1950. That's not the end of the world, but it is enough to not want to accentuate your losses during these corrections. We will need to be mindful of these dips.

Second, the markets have a history of crashing every seven to eight years. Here are some of the larger market crashes since 1900:

1903 - Rich Man's Panic (-22%)
1906 - General panic (-34%)
1911 - WWI and influenza (-51%)
1929 - Great Depression (-79%)
1937 - WWII (-50%)
1946 - Postwar bear market (-37%)
1961 - Cold War/Cuban Missile Crisis (-23%)
1966 - Recession (-22%)
1968 - Inflation bear market (-36%)
1972 - Inflation, Vietnam War and Watergate (-52%)
1980 - Stagflation (-27%)
1987 - Black Monday (-30%)
1990 - Iraq invaded Kuwait (-20%)
2000 - Dot-com crash (-49%)
2007 - Housing crisis (-56%)
2020 - COVID-19 pandemic (-34%)

The takeaway is that if your retirement is expected to last 30 years or so, you'll want to consider being prepared for experiencing potentially three to four market crashes. Again, this is why we fill the Principal Guaranteed Reservoir™.

Lastly, since 1900, there's been an interesting pattern of a grand scale. Every 20 years or so, the markets have gone flat for an extended period of time. Here is the data:

1909-1921 (13-year flat market cycle)
1922-1928 (7-year up market cycle)

1929-1944 (16-year flat market cycle)
1945-1964 (20 up market cycle)
1965-1974 (10-year flat market cycle)
1975-1999 (25-year up market cycle)
2000-2010 (11-year flat cycle)
2011- (Unknown up market cycle)

No one knows the future, but there is a reasonable argument to want to prepare for a flat market cycle if you expect your retirement to last 30 years. Because of these large-scale cycles, we need to be very deliberate in our investment and product decisions. Many retirees cannot afford to keep up with inflation if their investments make nothing for ten years. No one believes it could happen until it does.

There's no such thing as a perfect investment. Also, there's no such thing as a perfect investment strategy. That's why, before we dive into a conversation about investments and products, I want to introduce you to the Principle of Diversification, which suggests that you diversify your assets by objectives instead of lumping everything together with investment ambiguity.

As we just established, it may not be in your best interest to put everything at risk and hope it grows enough to solve all your problems. We need to have a plan for when the markets are up, down, or in a flat market cycle. That means we need to have different investments and products that can serve different purposes based on different market conditions.

I want to start by discussing your Principal Guaranteed Reservoir™ options. Later, I'll bring additional context into the picture so you can understand how to take your plan and create the Principal Guaranteed Reservoir™ that suits you and your preferences. Then, I want to introduce you to something called Absolute Return theory and Probability Investment Models™. The short explanation is they are models designed to make money in up, down, or flat markets. These models are risk models, as in they can lose money. Don't skip ahead. We will cover them. However, we must first discuss the Principal Guaranteed Reservoir™.

THE PRINCIPAL GUARANTEED RESERVOIR™ OPTIONS

The Principal Guaranteed Reservoir™ strategy suggests that when you retire or when you are near retirement you place a reasonable amount of assets within your lifestyle portfolio into one of the four accounts that offer reasonable growth potential and principal protection. Because these assets lack significant liquidity, it is important to know what you are getting into.

Essentially, there are two ways these accounts can grow. They can grow based on a fixed rate, like a Treasury, CD, or fixed annuity. Or, they can grow based on external indexes, like fixed-indexed annuities and fixed-indexed universal life insurance. Let's quickly review each of the options.

U.S. Treasuries

U.S. Treasuries work best if you buy them and hold them to maturity. If you were to sell them early, you could lose principal due to interest rate risk. Typically, when markets go down, interest rates also go down to try and help the market recover. When interest rates go down, U.S. Treasuries and other fixed-income products increase in value. This is why I am not as concerned about the possibility that you may end up selling them earlier than expected. I just want to be candid about the risk.

Treasuries tend to offer the least competitive rates but have the best liquidity. That's why, if there are significant income needs for the next five years, then you may consider using U.S. Treasuries as a part of your reservoir. Don't worry, once we finish the explanation of each of the reservoir options, I'll pull the plan back up and explain how you could assemble and fund your reservoir.

CDs

Bank CDs are probably the simplest of the bunch. You put funds in for a period of time. Once it matures, you get the funds back at the promised rate. If you need to liquidate a CD early, there is usually a small but manageable penalty, maybe three months' interest or so. CD rates can be tricky. Today's rates are no indicator of what rates will be like in five years.

Typically, those who use CDs are locking in expected returns for a specific time and place. For example, maybe you decide you want to retire in two years and you want to make sure that your first year of income is set. You may consider placing enough money into a two-year CD so once it matures, your first year of income is ready to go, regardless of market conditions.

Fixed Annuities

Fixed annuities offer a fixed interest rate for a certain amount of time. Many fixed annuities also allow you to take out 10%

of the account value without a surrender penalty (although you will be subject to income taxes and a 10% IRS penalty if you're under age 59 ½. Rates vary, so make sure you shop around. As a general rule, CDs are bank products for a defined period of time, whereas an annuity is designed to be a long-term retirement income product.

Remember, even though all annuities are designed to become income streams, the Principal Guaranteed Reservoir™ strategy suggests that you do not annuitize them. Once you have completed the surrender schedule, which is the schedule of illiquidity, the annuity continues to have growth potential while being 100% liquid. Don't forget it will still be subject to taxes.

Fixed-Indexed Annuities

Fixed-indexed annuities, or FIAs, have the potential to earn interest tied to the performance of an external market index while never being invested in the market or index itself. If the selected index goes up on the contract anniversary, you can benefit by having interest credited to your FIA. The interest (growth) will be subjected to certain limits based on how the company structures the product, as explained in the contract. Let's take this one step at a time.

First, it is important to understand something called the annual reset feature. Essentially, it means, every year, if you earn interest, the FIA value locks in a new "floor." Let me walk you through how this works.

Let's say you put $100,000 into an FIA that has a 50% participation rate. In year one, the index grew by 10%. The

$100,000 earns interest based on that 50% of the linked market index increase.

In other words, you would be credited 5% (10% x 50% = 5%). The annual reset establishes a new floor of $105,000. That means no matter what the market does, the contract value will be at least $105,000. The index that the FIA is tied to also has a new starting point.

Whatever the index is on the day the new floor is established is the new starting point. From that point, if the index goes up on your contract anniversary, your account balance can grow. If the index goes down, your account value would stay the same. The only way your account balance would go down is if you withdrew money from the account, or if you purchased optional features that involved an annual cost, which will still be deducted from the annuity value each year.

Now, let's say the index tanked in year two and lost 30%. Since the account had a new floor of $105,000, the annuity value remains at $105,000. It does not lose money.

To bring this home, let's say in year three, the index increases by 5% resulting in a 2.5% credit to the contract. (50% x 5% = 2.5%). So, the FIA is now worth $107,625.

Next, let's discuss the three ways indexed interest can be calculated and credited. First, by applying a cap rate. A cap means that if the index is up, you get interest credits equal to all the index growth up to a certain point (the cap rate). For example, if you have a cap rate of 5% and the index goes up 10%, your annuity would be credited 5%. If the index went up 2%, you would get 2%. That particular year did not exceed the cap rate, so your account was credited all of the growth. If the index went up 10%, you would only be credited 5%, because you are capped at 5%.

Second, they can have a spread. A spread means that if the index is up, you get interest equal to everything above a certain return. For example, if you have a spread of 4% and the index went up by 10%, your annuity would be credited interest of 6%. If the market was up by 20%, your annuity could earn 16%. If the market was up by 4%, your annuity would not earn anything. You receive interest credits from index gains that have exceeded the spread rate.

Third, they can have a participation rate. A participation rate means that if the index is up, you get interest tied to a percentage of the index gain. Like in the original example, if you had a 50% participation rate and the index was up by 10%, your annuity would be credited interest of 5%.

It's important to note, too, that an annuity may be limited by any one of these or a combination of these factors. For example, an FIA may have both a cap and a participation rate applied. It is crucial to understand the details of the contract. Know the benefits and the detriments before purchasing any product or investing in any investment.

Indexed Universal Life Insurance

A cash value life insurance policy known as "indexed universal life," or "IUL", is the last option for your reservoir.

While it should be purchased primarily for the death benefit it provides, whether that is for legacy purposes or to help the surviving spouse, it also has a cash value feature that you can access. Interest credited (growth) to the policy's cash value is similar to a fixed-indexed annuity, but it has many additional layers of complexity. As with all life insurance products, the primary reason for purchasing it is the death benefit for your beneficiaries. You will pay insurance charges for insuring your life, so it's important that you have a clear need for the coverage. You could use it to help support the surviving spouse to maintain their quality of life with a possible cash bump. It could also be used for estate planning purposes. The list goes on, but in the end, this is life insurance and should be used as such.

Life insurance has fees. How you rate, both medically and financially, will affect those fees. It is important to understand how those fees can play a role within the policy. Sometimes, the fees and costs can be too high for it to make sense to proceed with the policy. It's all about running the numbers and asking the right questions.

Aside from the death benefit feature, cash value life insurance offers additional benefits as well. Simply put, you can pay after-tax premiums, above and beyond what is needed to pay for the cost of insurance, and those funds can accumulate tax deferred. When used correctly, your cash value life insurance policy can be a source of tax-free income that settles up when you pass and the death benefit kicks in. Also, taking withdrawals from the policy's cash value will decrease the death benefits and cash value, and could cause the policy to lapse or require additional premiums to keep it in force. I'll explain more about how this can happen in a moment.

These policies offer a death benefit, principal protection, reasonable growth potential, and a reasonable level of liquidity in the policy's early years. Does it sound like the perfect financial vehicle? To some, maybe. However, when you look at its fees and unique potential tax characteristics, the list of detriments starts to stack up quickly.

As I mentioned, cash value life insurance has fees and charges for insuring you, so this will detract from the policy's overall performance. The majority of costs involved are typically found when you maintain a higher death benefit, or you are not in good health. Many times, there could be higher fees because the policy was not built efficiently, or if you purchase additional features and riders.

Life insurance is also one of the few assets that if not designed and managed correctly, it can blow up and cause a significant tax bill. It's called "MEC'ing" a policy. (MEC stands for a Modified Endowment Contract, which means that the IRS has determined that the policy is no longer classified solely as insurance due to the amount of premiums paid. They consider it an investment and will tax you differently). If you want to look more into this unique characteristic of cash value life insurance, look up modified endowment contracts online. I'd recommend checking out Investopedia as they have a great explainer video on Modified Endowment Contracts.

It can be complicated, so it is best discussed with a knowledgeable financial professional. There are plenty of safeguards in place but you need to manage your policy carefully so that you don't fall into this trap.

SELECTING YOUR PRINCIPAL GUARANTEED RESERVOIR™ OPTIONS

Now that we know what we can pick, let's have another look at the sample plan.

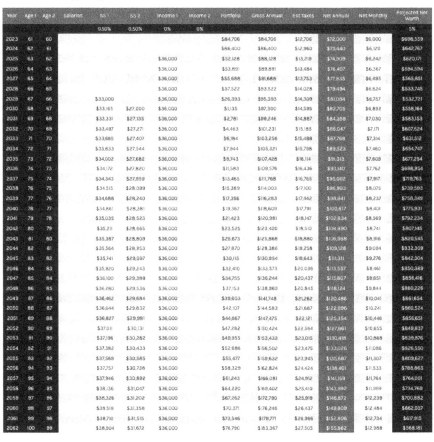

Year	Age 1	Age 2	Salaries	SS 1	SS 2	Income 1	Income 2	Portfolio	Gross Annual	Est Taxes	Net Annual	Net Monthly	Projected Net Worth
				0.50%	0.50%	0%	0%						5%
2023	61	60						$84,706	$84,706	$12,706	$72,000	$6,000	$698,559
2024	62	61						$86,400	$86,400	$12,960	$73,440	$6,120	$642,767
2025	63	62					$36,000	$52,128	$88,128	$13,219	$74,909	$6,242	$620,171
2026	64	63					$36,000	$53,891	$89,891	$13,484	$76,407	$6,367	$594,594
2027	65	64					$36,000	$55,688	$91,688	$13,753	$77,935	$6,495	$565,851
2028	66	65					$36,000	$57,522	$93,522	$14,028	$79,494	$6,624	$533,745
2029	67	66		$33,000			$36,000	$26,393	$95,393	$14,309	$81,084	$6,757	$532,721
2030	68	67		$33,165	$27,000	$36,000		$1,135	$97,300	$14,595	$82,705	$6,892	$558,164
2031	69	68		$33,331	$27,135	$36,000		$2,781	$99,246	$14,887	$84,359	$7,030	$583,153
2032	70	69		$33,497	$27,271	$36,000		$4,463	$101,231	$15,185	$86,047	$7,171	$607,624
2033	71	70		$33,665	$27,407	$36,000		$6,184	$103,256	$15,488	$87,768	$7,314	$631,512
2034	72	71		$33,833	$27,544	$36,000		$7,944	$105,321	$15,798	$89,523	$7,460	$654,747
2035	73	72		$34,002	$27,682	$36,000		$9,743	$107,428	$16,114	$91,313	$7,609	$677,234
2036	74	73		$34,172	$27,820	$36,000		$11,583	$109,576	$16,436	$93,140	$7,762	$698,954
2037	75	74		$34,343	$27,959	$36,000		$13,465	$111,768	$16,765	$95,002	$7,917	$719,763
2038	76	75		$34,515	$28,099	$36,000		$15,389	$114,003	$17,100	$96,903	$8,075	$739,593
2039	77	76		$34,688	$28,240	$36,000		$17,356	$116,283	$17,442	$98,841	$8,237	$758,349
2040	78	77		$34,861	$28,381	$36,000		$19,367	$118,609	$17,791	$100,817	$8,401	$775,931
2041	79	78		$35,035	$28,523	$36,000		$21,423	$120,981	$18,147	$102,834	$8,569	$792,234
2042	80	79		$35,211	$28,665	$36,000		$23,525	$123,400	$18,510	$104,890	$8,741	$807,145
2043	81	80		$35,387	$28,809	$36,000		$25,673	$125,868	$18,880	$106,988	$8,916	$820,545
2044	82	81		$35,564	$28,953	$36,000		$27,870	$128,386	$19,258	$109,128	$9,094	$832,309
2045	83	82		$35,741	$29,097	$36,000		$30,115	$130,954	$19,643	$111,311	$9,276	$842,304
2046	84	83		$35,920	$29,243	$36,000		$32,410	$133,573	$20,036	$113,537	$9,461	$850,389
2047	85	84		$36,100	$29,389	$36,000		$34,755	$136,244	$20,437	$115,807	$9,651	$856,416
2048	86	85		$36,280	$29,536	$36,000		$37,153	$138,969	$20,845	$118,124	$9,844	$860,226
2049	87	86		$36,462	$29,684	$36,000		$39,603	$141,748	$21,262	$120,486	$10,041	$861,654
2050	88	87		$36,644	$29,832	$36,000		$42,107	$144,583	$21,687	$122,896	$10,241	$860,524
2051	89	88		$36,827	$29,981	$36,000		$44,667	$147,475	$22,121	$125,354	$10,446	$856,651
2052	90	89		$37,011	$30,131	$36,000		$47,282	$150,424	$22,564	$127,861	$10,655	$848,837
2053	91	90		$37,196	$30,282	$36,000		$48,955	$153,433	$23,015	$130,418	$10,868	$839,876
2054	92	91		$37,382	$30,433	$36,000		$52,686	$156,502	$23,475	$133,026	$11,086	$826,550
2055	93	92		$37,569	$30,585	$36,000		$55,477	$159,632	$23,945	$135,687	$11,307	$809,627
2056	94	93		$37,757	$30,738	$36,000		$58,329	$162,824	$24,424	$138,401	$11,533	$788,863
2057	95	94		$37,946	$30,892	$36,000		$61,243	$166,081	$24,912	$141,169	$11,764	$764,001
2058	96	95		$38,136	$31,047	$36,000		$64,220	$169,402	$25,410	$143,992	$11,999	$734,769
2059	97	96		$38,326	$31,202	$36,000		$67,262	$172,790	$25,919	$146,872	$12,239	$700,882
2060	98	97		$38,518	$31,358	$36,000		$70,371	$176,246	$26,437	$149,809	$12,484	$662,037
2061	99	98		$38,710	$31,515	$36,000		$73,546	$179,771	$26,966	$152,806	$12,734	$617,915
2062	100	99		$38,904	$31,672	$36,000		$76,790	$183,367	$27,505	$155,862	$12,988	$568,181

Hypothetical illustration shown for demonstration purposes only. It is not guaranteed and not indicative of your actual plan results.

Notice how in the first two years in the portfolio income column, if the markets were to crash, you'd need around $84,000 to $86,000 liquid and ready to go from your reservoir. Because that is a significant withdrawal from the portfolio (over 10%), you might want to consider short-term treasuries or CDs. Don't chance it. Consider creating a mini U.S. Treasury or CD ladder so you don't have to stress as much about the markets.

Next, look at the following four years. They would need around $50,000 of income if the markets were to crash. That's too short of a time frame to consider an annuity or cash value life insurance, so it may be another $50,000 in treasuries.

At this point, we would have around $160,000 laddered for income for year one and year two, plus another $50,000 in case there is a multi-year bear market, or a second market crash happens sooner than expected.

Do you notice how the plan is shaping our allocation decisions?

Once Social Security kicks in, we have very little need for a reservoir. If we assume two more crashes in retirement, then we could look at a more long-term solution, like a fixed-indexed annuity or, if you were healthy enough, perhaps a small indexed-universal life insurance policy, assuming you also want the death benefit. The total additional amount of the portfolio that could go to finish funding the Principal Guaranteed Reservoir™ would be around $60,000. I took the average of how much is coming out of the portfolio, starting when Social Security turns on and going all the way to age 100, and got around $20,000. Now assume that there could be another three market crashes, that's three times $20,000 and you got $60,000. Sure, the account will grow, but that growth can help prepare for a fourth crash if that were to happen.

Based on this situation, this person could consider taking their $750,000 and allocating $280,000 to their Principal Guaranteed Portfolio™ and significantly decrease their overall retirement risk.

What we did had nothing to do with generic guidance, like a 60/40 slip, or the rule of 100, if you've heard of it, and so on. It was all incredibly deliberate, based on a plan.

Most people know how to shop for U.S. Treasuries and CDs. However, if you want to shop for fixed or fixed-index annuities, and/or cash value life insurance, you will have to go to a licensed insurance professional. They are usually not available as an "over-the-counter" product.

I want to share a few words of warning about insurance products. Many annuities I have seen over the years, for example, have had horrible returns. It's almost like, no matter what's going on or how they are built, they all want to target a 3% or a 4% return. Not all are like that, but many seem to be, based on my observations over the past decade. Here are some tips to consider in case you want a few annuities for your reservoir.

Tip #1: Only work with an independent advisor or independent insurance agent when considering your options.

I've got nothing against State Farm, New York Life, or your local bank/credit union. My only concern is that they can only sell what their company offers. An independent advisor or independent insurance agent can search for the right products through their wholesaler relationships, so you can find and purchase the right products for your situation.

Tip #2: Proceed with caution when presented with a new index.

If you are considering an indexed PG Account, whether it's a fixed-indexed annuity or life insurance policy, there's a good chance that you'll be presented with a new product featuring a new index. New indexes are, in my opinion and experience, like putting lipstick on a pig.

A few months ago, I was helping another advisor vet a product he wanted to offer his clients. He said it was the best annuity he had seen. "The historicals are incredible!" I became increasingly suspicious.

When I looked at the historicals reflected in the illustration, the new index had never lost money. Even in 2008, it had allegedly made money. Sure, it was possible to have made money in 2008. However, it was not probable for a generic index to have done so. I then did a quick search and found that this index was currently down significantly, year to date, when the market was relatively flat.

Doesn't it seem strange that an index, which was so well built that it allegedly made money in 2008, was significantly down during a flat year? I then discovered that this index was created in 2015. It was cherry-picked data. The index started falling apart once the market started experiencing difficult times.

Unfortunately, this is not an uncommon situation. I could tell story after story about how conducting a little due diligence can help cut through the fantastic marketing material and expose the facts about the index options and products.

I generally recommend that consumers look for the indices they know and are comfortable with, like the S&P 500®. If you are open to alternative indices, make sure there's a sufficient amount of due diligence done and that it passes the "sniff test."

Tip #3: Watch out for teaser rates.

Many Fixed-Indexed PG Accounts offer higher participation rates that only last a few years. An insurance company's reputation is an important intangible data point when considering a product. You don't want your rate to drop significantly when the product is out of the surrender charge period.

Tip #4: Avoid products that take more than two years to lock in interest.

One of the crucial features of insurance-based Fixed-Indexed PG Accounts is that every year, or every other year, you can lock in a new "floor." As a quick refresher, after a year, any interest credited is locked in and a new floor is established. From that point on, if the markets crash, you don't lose money below that newly established floor. The educational simulation shared previously showed interest being locked in every year.

Some products will try to tempt you with better possible returns and higher caps, lower spreads, or higher participation rates if you accept a contract that takes longer to lock in interest. I've seen some that take as long as five years before a new floor is locked in. In my experience, the longer it takes to lock in the interest, the greater risk you may have. A bad year or two could wipe out any positive gains of the index, resulting in little to no growth over a longer time period.

Consider the fact that, according to the Motley Fool, the market averages a -10% correction or worse every 1.8 years[2]. Sure, you can bounce back from these dips, but we can't control when they hit and how fast the recovery is. We are at the mercy of the market. If the correction occurs at the wrong time, you could lose out on any interest credited to your Fixed-Indexed PG Account.

Don't get greedy.

When I recommend fixed-index annuities or life insurance policies, it almost always has an annual reset where credited interest is locked in and a new floor is set every year. On rare occasions, a two-year reset (a new floor every two years) may make sense when potential growth is connected to an index that can dynamically rebalance. Even then, proceed with caution.

In the end, it is important to work with someone you trust and respect. They must be willing to do the due diligence for you and then present the most appropriate products to you.

As a quick aside, please note that cash value life insurance has too many variables to properly discuss within this book. It would be appropriate to discuss with an independent advisor or independent insurance agent about your specific situation. They have a lot to offer. Make sure you know the detriments.

If I had one big takeaway to offer you here, it would be to focus on products that offer the specific features you're looking for along with the most potential returns. Once you have those products picked out, then make sure to organize the liquidity timelines and ladder them out as needed.

Now it's time to talk about what to do with the rest of the portfolio.

ABSOLUTE RETURN AND PROBABILITY INVESTMENT MODELS™

I'll never forget what my banker told me when he found out I worked in finance. He pulled me close and said, "Look, I know we both work in finance, but let's be real. Just buy these two indexes and you're fine, right?" I couldn't believe my ears.

It's true, that for the plan to work, you can use passive investments. Buy investments that mirror the indexes (because you can't actually invest in the index itself), hopefully more than just two, and ride the markets up and down. You may be able to afford to do that because if or when the markets go down, you have your Principal Guaranteed Reservoir™ ready to go, assuming it was set up correctly.

Passive investments, buying the index's components, and other similar strategies are all based on a relative return. If you buy SPX, for example, you're not literally buying the S&P 500®. You are buying a fund that holds S&P 500® positions and tries to match its returns.

What most people have not heard of is a term called *absolute return*. Its goal is to make money, regardless of market conditions. Typically, absolute return models can be found in hedge funds and large endowments. As I write these words, Absolute Return is the largest allocation within the Yale Endowment fund.

These models are incredibly hard to come by, especially when you consider their track record. Kedrec is among the few that offer absolute return models to the general public, as in you don't have to have multiple millions to qualify. I want to take a moment and explain them so you are aware of how they work. It's okay if you never become a client. At least you know they exist. We call our models Probability Investment Models™.

Probability Investment Models™

Imagine you put the top 400 stocks of the S&P 500® on a bench plus the option of going to cash. Then, every day, you ran an algorithm that looked at their various moving average indicators, a history of behavioral patterns, current trends within the sector of the stock, and so on. Basically, think of the stock getting a physical every night.

Once the data is complete, the top ten with the highest probability of success, based on the algorithms, are pulled from the bench and invested. They are expected to be there for a predetermined amount of time, based on their historical patterns. This is technical analysis on steroids.

There's no emotion, no trying to outsmart the market, and especially no trying to read the tea leaves. It is rules-based investing. The goal is typically to match the index plus two percent while going to cash during the downtrends. Remember, cash is on the bench and is an option at any point. Cash is king in down markets, which is why it must always be an option.

It would not be appropriate to go any deeper into the topic in this book. Remember, passive investing and other types of investing can work as well. Just make sure you fund your Principal Guaranteed Reservoir™.

If you want to learn more about our Probability Investment Models™, my team is here to answer any questions you may have. Just go to www.kedrec.com/call. If you do schedule a call, please note that it's always okay to say "no." We do not believe in high-pressure situations. If you schedule a call and decide it's not for you, we are not going to keep calling you. That's a waste of everyone's time. We only want to work with those who want to work with us and want to implement the services (like these models) we offer.

SELECTING YOUR STRATEGIES CONCLUSION

Notice how everything we discussed was guided by the plan. Notice how each investment decision was based on systems, algorithms, principles, and rules. When emotions play a role, returns are often compromised. The emotion of fear tends to keep people out of the market longer than they should be. The emotion of greed tends to keep people in the market longer than they should be.

Don't let your emotions compromise your ability to retire on time and stay retired.

Write down what your portfolio needs to look like moving forward and how you intend to bring it to life. Sometimes, you can transition into your new retirement portfolio within a month. Other times, because of capital gains issues, assets stuck in a 401(k), and so on, it can take several years. Regardless of the situation, start deliberately putting your portfolio together.

I'll see you in the next chapter.

Chapter 8

HOW TO RETIRE ON TIME AND STAY RETIRED

"There's no such thing as bad weather, only unsuitable clothing."

– Alfred Wainwright

By this point, you should have a Functional Wealth Plan™ that is close to where you want it. You should also have a rough idea of how to fund your retirement portfolio, based on your plan. The last question to answer is, what do you do once the plan and portfolio are funded?

This chapter is intended to help you understand how to maintain your plan. As I mentioned before, I honestly believe that with the right plan, supported by the right portfolio, most people should be able to manage their retirement on their own. It's time to show you how to manage your plan and portfolio so regardless of market conditions, you can keep income coming in without accentuating your losses.

THE FUNCTIONAL WEALTH PLAN™ INCOME PLAYBOOK

How you manage your assets will change over time. For example, when you first retire, IRA to Roth conversions may be more important to you than when you are in your late 70s. Each income play has its place. If markets are down, you take income from your Principal Guaranteed Reservoir™. If markets are up, pick one of the plays to execute, based on your goals.

Ready?

Let's begin.

The Max Tax Play

The Max Tax Play is what I call it when you set a max tax amount, take 100% of your income from pre-tax accounts, and use the rest as IRA to Roth conversions. The idea here is to basically set a limit or maximum amount of pre-tax distributions for one year or multiple years. Instead of maxing out your bracket, you set your max limit on your terms. We will go through a simple tax assessment later in the book. For now, try to learn the principles behind the strategies.

Let's say, for example, your max limit is $150,000 and you have an effective tax rate of 20%. That means you would expect to pull $150,000 from pre-tax accounts for one year or several years, pay around $30,000 in income tax, and then split between how much your income is and how much you can convert. Here's an oversimplified breakdown to try and help illustrate this play.

Year 1:
- Max Tax: $150,000
- Taxes: $30,000
- Net Income: $100,000
- Net Conversion: $20,000

"Net Conversion" means the amount, after taxes are paid, that actually went into the tax-free account (e.g., Roth IRA).

Year 2:
- Max Tax: $150,000
- Taxes: $30,000
- Net Income: $102,000
- Net Conversion: $18,000

Year 3:
- Max Tax: $150,000
- Taxes: $30,000
- Net Income: $105,000
- Net Conversion: $15,000

Hypothetical example shown for illustrative purposes only.

The theory behind this play is to determine how much you are willing to pay in taxes over the next few years. Now you know what you can roughly expect each year while you enjoy your income and convert the leftovers from pre-tax accounts to tax-free accounts. This means you pay taxes on the converted funds now so that they can be accessed tax-free later in retirement. Do not start this until after age 59 ½. You do not want to pay additional penalties by taking funds out incorrectly before the age of 59 ½.

The play is usually more appropriate when current tax rates seem like they will be lower than in the near future. Typically, this strategy would be used between when someone retires and the age of 65 (before they file for Medicare). If you are 65 or older, make sure you watch out for the Medicare Income-Related Monthly Adjustment Amount, or IRMAA. When you take too much income from taxable sources, you can trigger an increase in your Medicare Premiums.

Typically, this strategy can be used to help minimize future tax burdens fast.

The Minimalist Play

The Minimalist Play, as I call it, only works once you have converted enough of your assets from pre-tax accounts to tax-free accounts. This play typically shows up later in your plan.

To execute this play, you will first determine how much pre-tax income you can take without putting yourself into the next tax bracket. That includes your Social Security benefit, your pension (if you have one), and any other income stream that may trigger taxes. Once you have established your taxable income limit from pre-tax accounts, you then take the rest from your tax-free accounts.

Some people will be able to implement the Minimalist Play within the lowest tax bracket, depending on their Social Security benefit. Those who have pensions or other taxable income streams may find themselves in the second or third lowest tax bracket when implementing this play, and that's okay. This play can vary significantly, based on your unique situation.

The Buffet Play

I'm not talking about Warren Buffett. I'm talking about a literal buffet, like where you'd go for lunch or dinner. When you arrive, it's hard not to take a little bit of everything, right? The purpose of this play is to take a little from all three tax account types (pre-tax, after-tax, and tax-free) while trying to keep the total tax liabilities to a minimum.

In addition, you try to take a little from all types of accounts, including your Principal Guaranteed Reservoir™. It is possible to have too big of a reservoir. Your long-term goals are probably better suited in the market where there is more growth potential.

HOW TO STAY RETIRED EXERCISES

When a kid gets their driver's license, it means they have proven to the DMV that they know how to drive, technically speaking. That doesn't mean they are any good at it. It means they understand how to start a car and get from point A to point B with a reasonable chance of not crashing. There's something to be said about having "time in the saddle." The same could be said about managing your plan and portfolio.

We've covered the principles, framework, and strategies enough to be considered dangerous. Now, it's time to put them to the test. Consider the rest of this chapter your driver's test. Let's run a few hypothetical scenarios to see if the principles make enough sense that you would be able to correctly apply them.

Please note that even if you pass this casual test, remember, it's okay to still be a little nervous. Admittedly, it could take years of time in the saddle before you start to feel comfortable managing and maintaining your plan and portfolio.

Let's begin.

Scenario 1: The market crashes 35% in the second year of your retirement. Where do you pull your income?

Answer: You would pull your portfolio income from the Principal Guaranteed Reservoir™. After a year has passed, you verify whether or not your accounts have recovered. If they did recover, then all would be well, and you could pull income from anywhere.

If your other accounts did not recover, as was the case for many in 2000, 2001, and 2002, then you would keep taking income from your Principal Guaranteed Reservoir™ so that you don't compromise your other accounts. Remember, you don't want to accentuate your losses.

Scenario 2: You're turning 65 years old and you still have a significant amount of money in pre-tax accounts. Do you keep converting the maximum amount of Traditional IRA assets to Roth IRAs while staying within your current tax bracket?

Answer: The answer is it depends. However, as a general rule, once you turn 65, you want to keep your income tax as low as possible so that you don't increase your Medicare premiums. Consider setting your Max Tax Play limit just below IRMAA, if possible.

Scenario 3: The market had an incredible year. Where should you pull your income?

Answer: This is a trick question. You can pull income from any investment group. However, when markets have been up, it is generally more efficient to pull income from different accounts in order to help minimize future tax liabilities. This means it may be in your best interest to pull from your risk accounts and your reservoir. Also, you may want to pull from your pre-tax accounts and your after-tax accounts to help minimize your overall tax burdens. It's a balancing act to maximize income while trying to keep tax liabilities low.

Scenario 4: My accounts have done well for the past few years. I want to spend as much as I can since I don't plan on leaving anything to my kids. Can I increase my income?

Answer: Over the span of five to ten years, it is expected that some years may exceed expectations while other years may underperform. Subtle adjustments after five years or so may be appropriate. Anything less than five years may not be appropriate.

If you start with two good years, and then increase your income, you may be spreading yourself too thin when you get to the third year. If the third year lacks sufficient performance, it could really hurt your plan. Do not get greedy. Stick to the plan and expectations that were originally set. Most of all, maintain the necessary liquidity in your Principal Guaranteed Reservoir™.

Scenario 5: I've been retired for ten years now. My Principal Guaranteed Reservoir™ has gone down significantly. Should I put more into my reservoir?

Answer: It's hard to offer a definitive answer, but as a general rule, it is okay to have less in your reservoir over time. Your risk accounts are expected to eventually dwarf your reservoir.
One of the few times you may consider putting additional assets in your reservoir would be if you have been pulling income from them exclusively over the past few years due to poor market performance. This could happen if you were to retire at the beginning of a flat market cycle.

Scenario 6: How often should I review my estate plan?

Answer: It is a good idea to have your estate plan reviewed and updated every two to three years. Laws change. If your estate plan is not updated, it may lead to discrepancies that prevent your intentions from being fulfilled.

Scenario 7: I'm getting bored in retirement. What should I do?

Answer: Get a part-time job. Go volunteer. Find religion. If single, consider dating. Search until you find purpose. You must have a reason to get up in the morning. If you don't, research shows that you will cognitively decline at a faster rate.

Unless you have a purpose in retirement, it may not be worth it. The "vacation" honeymoon phase of retirement usually only lasts a year. Once the honeymoon phase is done, depression can set in. Do not let that happen to you.

Many people reinvent themselves in retirement. Do whatever it takes, but find purpose. Retirement is meant to be a good time, not a lonely time.

In Conclusion

As I wrap up this chapter, I want to invite you to consider other scenarios that may concern you. There are an infinite number of situations that can cause you to lose sleep. Dwelling on them with a spirit of procrastination won't bring you peace. You'll need to take action in order to find a solution. Running through those situations now can help you be prepared for if or when they happen. Keep doing these exercises until you feel confident about the idea of retirement. Remember, your retirement is for you. Don't retire for someone else.

Part 3

THE LIFESTYLE PORTFOLIO ALIGNMENT

Chapter 9

WHICH PORTFOLIO DESIGN SUITS YOU?

"If you fail to plan, you are planning to fail."

– Benjamin Franklin

My favorite interviewing question is, "Do you love to win or hate to lose?" Both answers are in agreement with the overall goal, to win. However, it forces you to pick a perspective and ultimately a priority for your portfolio. This chapter is intended to help you find what is most important to you and design your portfolio accordingly.

This entire book focuses on how to build a custom Functional Wealth Plan™ while following the principles of retirement. There are so many ways you could create your plan and still follow the principles. Some scenarios could offer more growth potential while others can offer more protection.

Remember, there's no such thing as a perfect investment. It is important to follow the Principle of Diversification and deliberately allocate your assets, based on your financial goals and objectives.

Instead of leaving you with an overgeneralized direction, I want to take a moment and walk you through a few exercises to help dial in what your portfolio could look like. I do not want you stuck with "blank page syndrome." So, let's take your first step into what could be right for you.

Below, you will find two self-guided assessments. The first assessment is intended to help you determine which is more important to you: growth potential or protection. If you were to pick growth potential over protection, it doesn't mean that you don't want protection. It means growth potential is more important to you when you consider your long-term goals. The same is true if you were to pick protection over growth potential.

The second self-guided assessment attempts to understand which is more important to you: flexibility or structure. Some people want to know as many details as they can about their plan and what to expect. They don't do well when plans change. However, others prefer to be able to adjust and evolve over time. Both are possible to accomplish while following the principles and strategies found within this book. Hence, we want to find out which you prefer.

Here is roughly what the outcome could look like:

	Structure	Flexibility
Protection	Protection + Structure	Protection + Flexibility
Growth Potential	Growth Potential + Structure	Growth Potential + Flexibility

Once we find out your preferences, we can dive deeper into how to build a portfolio that is suited for you. For years, suitability questions were, in my opinion, too vague. For example, you may be asked something like, "What is your risk tolerance? Conservative? Moderate? Aggressive?" I would always go back to these suitability questions and ask, "What does that even mean?" It felt like just words without context.

These assessments, with your plan, can help bring a significant amount of clarity in your retirement preparation. Remember, I want to teach you how to fish. I'll give a few examples after the assessment so you have additional context. Also, in the next chapter, we will run one last assessment to see how close you are to implementing the portfolio design that suits you.

Ready?

Let's do the first assessment.

GROWTH POTENTIAL VS. PROTECTION ASSESSMENT

Below, rate yourself on a scale from 0–5 on how accurate the statements are—0 means "not accurate at all," and 5 means "most accurate."

Once you've rated yourself for each statement, total up your scores and then use the Answer Key to determine which preference is more suited to you.

Portfolio Design Questions, Part 1	Self-Rating
I want to maximize the amount of money I can leave to my beneficiaries as a part of my legacy.	
I want to maximize my income.	
I am comfortable losing -30% to -40% every now and then if it means I have more overall upside potential throughout retirement.	
The daily fluctuations of the market do not bother me.	
Underperforming the market consistently is worse than the occasional market correction.	
I am more concerned about my account balances 10 years from now than what they will be next year.	
I tend to look at my accounts on an annual basis.	

WHICH PORTFOLIO DESIGN SUITS YOU?

WHAT YOUR SCORE REALLY MEANS

> **SCORE: 0-20**
> **PROTECTION**

You are more concerned about not losing your nest egg than trying to be the richest person in the graveyard. Preservation is a high priority. You may watch the markets and your accounts often and need to feel like you are not on the "Wall Street Rollercoaster". Slow and steady is better than fast and wild. If this sounds like you, then chances are protection is more important than growth. That doesn't mean you don't want growth. It means you don't want major ups and downs in your portfolio.

In a moment, we are going to bring it all together. Remember, if your score brought you here, then you fall into the Protection row.

	Structure	Flexibility
Protection	**Protection + Structure**	**Protection + Flexibility**
Growth Potential	Growth Potential + Structure	Growth Potential + Flexibility

> **SCORE: 21+**
> **GROWTH POTENTIAL**

No risk, no reward, right? The day-to-day doesn't bother you. It's about the big picture. You are comfortable with the ups and downs as long as there are more ups than downs. You've been doing this for a while and are comfortable with the behavior of the stock market. You know that markets can crash. Inside, you believe it's just a matter of time before markets recover, and you're willing to hang on. The only two prices that matter are the price you bought the investment and the price you sold it, right?

If this sounds like you then growth is probably more important to you than protection. That doesn't mean you want everything to be at risk. It means you want the most upside potential possible without getting too reckless.

In a moment, we are going to bring it all together. Remember, if your score brought you here, then you fall into the Growth Potential row.

	Structure	Flexibility
Protection	Protection + Structure	Protection + Flexibility
Growth Potential	**Growth Potential + Structure**	**Growth Potential + Flexibility**

Alright, now it is time to do the second assessment.

STRUCTURE VS. FLEXIBILITY ASSESSMENT

Below, rate yourself on a scale from 0–5 on how accurate the statements are—0 means "not accurate at all," and 5 means "most accurate."

Once you've rated yourself for each statement, total up your scores and then use the Answer Key to determine which preference is more suited to you.

Portfolio Design Questions, Part 2	Self-Rating
I like to have a plan in place that is predictable.	
I would prefer to know how much of my income should be expected in years 1, 5, and 10, and from where it is expected to come.	
I believe that if it is working, you should leave it alone.	
I do not like surprises, good or bad.	
I am stressed if I do not understand how something important works.	
I keep a strict budget and know where I spend every penny.	
I prefer routine over adventures.	

WHAT YOUR SCORE REALLY MEANS

SCORE: 0-20
FLEXIBILITY

If you want to make God laugh, tell him your plan. There's only so much you can do, so you might as well roll with the punches. You probably don't sweat the small stuff. As long as there's enough structure to have confidence that things will work out, that's enough for you. If this sounds like you, then chances are you prefer flexibility over structure.

In a moment, we are going to bring it all together. Remember, if your score brought you here, then you fall into the Flexibility column.

	Structure	**Flexibility**
Protection	Protection + Structure	**Protection + Flexibility**
Growth Potential	Growth Potential + Structure	**Growth Potential + Flexibility**

SCORE: 21+
STRUCTURE

Comfort is found in consistency and dependability. It is better to make a plan and stick to it than just wing it. The devil is in the details, which is why it is important to spend the time now so you do not end up in a reactive position later. If this sounds like you, chances are you prefer structure over flexibility.

In a moment, we are going to bring it all together. Remember, if your score brought you here, then you fall into the Structure column.

	Structure	Flexibility
Protection	**Protection + Structure**	Protection + Flexibility
Growth Potential	**Growth Potential + Structure**	Growth Potential + Flexibility

BRINGING IT ALL TOGETHER

Now it's time to discuss what each of those portfolios could look like.

Here is the chart, again. Based on how you answered, you should end up in one of the four options. Don't just read the portfolio design based on your results. Take a moment and read all four. You may end up deciding to blend these strategies together.

The Larger Traditional Reservoir

If your results were protection and flexibility, then the Larger Traditional Reservoir may be right for you. Here's what it would look like on the chart.

	Structure	**Flexibility**
Protection		**Protection + Flexibility**
Growth Potential		

The Larger Traditional Reservoir attempts to fill the entire reservoir needs at the beginning of retirement. When the markets crash, this version of the reservoir is intended to provide income until the markets recover and then some. Let's take a look at the example plan that we used earlier and bring context into the conversation.

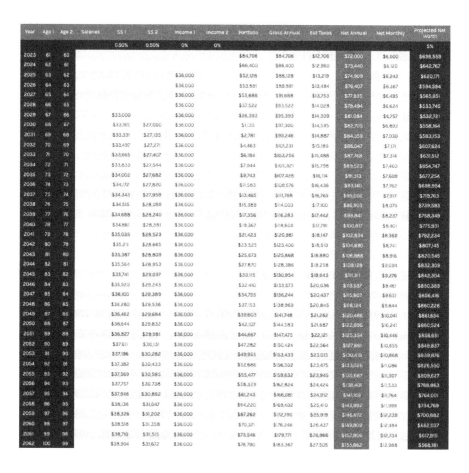

Year	Age 1	Age 2	Salaries	SS 1	SS 2	Income 1	Income 2	Portfolio	Gross Annual	Est Taxes	Net Annual	Net Monthly	Projected Net Worth
				0.50%	0.50%	0%	0%						5%
2023	61	60						$84,706	$84,706	$12,706	$72,000	$6,000	$698,559
2024	62	61						$86,400	$86,400	$12,960	$73,440	$6,120	$642,767
2025	63	62				$36,000		$52,128	$88,128	$13,219	$74,909	$6,242	$620,171
2026	64	63				$36,000		$53,591	$89,591	$13,484	$76,407	$6,367	$594,594
2027	65	64				$36,000		$55,688	$91,688	$13,753	$77,935	$6,495	$565,851
2028	66	65				$36,000		$57,522	$93,522	$14,028	$79,494	$6,624	$533,745
2029	67	66	$33,000			$36,000		$26,393	$95,393	$14,309	$81,084	$6,757	$532,721
2030	68	67	$33,165	$27,000		$36,000		$1,135	$97,300	$14,595	$82,705	$6,892	$558,164
2031	69	68	$33,331	$27,135		$36,000		$2,781	$99,246	$14,887	$84,359	$7,030	$583,153
2032	70	69	$33,497	$27,271		$36,000		$4,463	$101,231	$15,185	$86,047	$7,171	$607,624
2033	71	70	$33,665	$27,407		$36,000		$6,184	$103,256	$15,488	$87,768	$7,314	$631,512
2034	72	71	$33,833	$27,544		$36,000		$7,944	$105,321	$15,798	$89,523	$7,460	$654,747
2035	73	72	$34,002	$27,682		$36,000		$9,743	$107,428	$16,114	$91,313	$7,609	$677,254
2036	74	73	$34,172	$27,820		$36,000		$11,583	$108,576	$16,436	$93,140	$7,762	$698,954
2037	75	74	$34,343	$27,959		$36,000		$13,465	$111,768	$16,765	$95,002	$7,917	$719,763
2038	76	75	$34,515	$28,099		$36,000		$15,389	$114,003	$17,100	$96,903	$8,075	$739,593
2039	77	76	$34,688	$28,240		$36,000		$17,356	$116,283	$17,442	$98,841	$8,237	$758,349
2040	78	77	$34,861	$28,381		$36,000		$19,367	$118,608	$17,791	$100,817	$8,401	$775,931
2041	79	78	$35,035	$28,523		$36,000		$21,423	$120,981	$18,147	$102,834	$8,569	$792,234
2042	80	79	$35,211	$28,665		$36,000		$23,525	$123,400	$18,510	$104,890	$8,741	$807,145
2043	81	80	$35,387	$28,809		$36,000		$25,673	$125,868	$18,880	$106,988	$8,916	$820,545
2044	82	81	$35,564	$28,953		$36,000		$27,870	$128,386	$19,258	$109,128	$9,094	$832,309
2045	83	82	$35,741	$29,097		$36,000		$30,115	$130,954	$19,643	$111,311	$9,276	$842,304
2046	84	83	$35,920	$29,243		$36,000		$32,410	$133,573	$20,036	$113,537	$9,461	$850,389
2047	85	84	$36,100	$29,389		$36,000		$34,755	$136,244	$20,437	$115,807	$9,651	$856,416
2048	86	85	$36,280	$29,536		$36,000		$37,153	$138,969	$20,845	$118,124	$9,844	$860,226
2049	87	86	$36,462	$29,684		$36,000		$39,603	$141,748	$21,262	$120,486	$10,041	$861,654
2050	88	87	$36,644	$29,832		$36,000		$42,107	$144,583	$21,687	$122,896	$10,241	$860,524
2051	89	88	$36,527	$29,981		$36,000		$44,667	$147,475	$22,121	$125,354	$10,446	$856,651
2052	90	89	$37,011	$30,131		$36,000		$47,282	$150,424	$22,564	$127,861	$10,655	$849,837
2053	91	90	$37,196	$30,282		$36,000		$49,955	$153,433	$23,015	$130,418	$10,868	$839,876
2054	92	91	$37,382	$30,433		$36,000		$52,686	$156,502	$23,475	$133,026	$11,086	$826,550
2055	93	92	$37,569	$30,585		$36,000		$55,477	$159,632	$23,945	$135,687	$11,307	$809,627
2056	94	93	$37,757	$30,738		$36,000		$58,329	$162,824	$24,424	$138,401	$11,533	$788,863
2057	95	94	$37,946	$30,892		$36,000		$61,243	$166,081	$24,912	$141,168	$11,764	$764,001
2058	96	95	$38,136	$31,047		$36,000		$64,220	$169,402	$25,410	$143,992	$11,999	$734,769
2059	97	96	$38,326	$31,202		$36,000		$67,262	$172,790	$25,919	$146,872	$12,239	$700,882
2060	98	97	$38,518	$31,358		$36,000		$70,371	$176,246	$26,437	$149,809	$12,484	$662,037
2061	99	98	$38,710	$31,515		$36,000		$73,546	$179,771	$26,966	$152,806	$12,734	$617,915
2062	100	99	$38,904	$31,672		$36,000		$76,790	$183,367	$27,505	$155,862	$12,988	$568,181

Hypothetical illustration shown for demonstration purposes only. It is not guaranteed and not indicative of your actual plan results.

The idea is that if markets crash every seven to eight years, and we assume that it may take two to three years for a recovery, then we divide the plan up into sections and then make sure there is enough liquidity in the Principal Guaranteed Reservoir™ to help keep income coming in.

For example, take the first seven years of the plan. For the first two years, the plan suggests that you could need around $80,000 in income each year. Then, it drops down to around $50,000 for the next six years. So, for this section, you would take the three years with the largest amounts and use that number as a guide on how much needs to go into the reservoir. In this situation, it could be somewhere around $210,000 ($80,000 + $80,000 + $50,000).

Notice how in year seven of the plan, the income coming from the portfolio is around $1,000. As inflation increases, the income from the portfolio amount increases to around $50,000 later on in the plan. That means the second section and all subsequent sections would require a relatively small reservoir. You could consider around $25,000 to $50,000 to help cover future crashes later in the plan. Remember, the products that qualify for the Principal Guaranteed Reservoir™ offer growth potential and principal protection. They are expected to grow, not just sit around like what cash typically does.

Here is what it could look like, if we were to look at the portfolio through the pie chart lens.

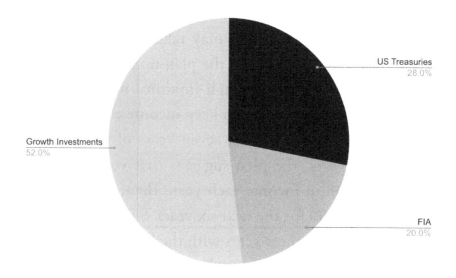

US Treasuries
28.0%

Growth Investments
52.0%

FIA
20.0%

Hypothetical illustration shown for demonstration purposes only. It is not guaranteed and not indicative of your actual plan results.

This portfolio is intended for someone who wants less overall risk exposure but still wants to maintain their flexibility. Over time, if the reservoir becomes bigger than necessary, it would be prudent to exclusively drain it slowly. You do not want more than is necessary in your reservoir because it can hinder overall growth potential.

The Smaller Traditional Reservoir

If your results were growth potential and flexibility, then the Smaller Traditional Reservoir may be right for you. Here's what it would look like on the chart.

	Structure	**Flexibility**
Protection		
Growth Potential		**Growth Potential + Flexibility**

The Smaller Traditional Reservoir is similar to the Larger Traditional Reservoir, except it is intended to allocate more assets to the accounts that have higher growth potential. If you consider the example before, it would follow the same philosophy, except allocate less to the Principal Guaranteed Reservoir™.

This portfolio design focuses on bearing the brunt of the market crash in the first year. Instead of taking three years of each section as a guide, you would only take one year. For example, $80,000 is roughly the largest amount during the first seven years. $11,000 is roughly the largest amount in the second seven-year section. $40,000 is roughly the largest amount in the third section. The growth and anything left over could be used for the fourth section. That brings the rough amount to be funded in the Principal Guaranteed Reservoir™ to around $131,000.

Here is what this example could look like in the form of a pie chart.

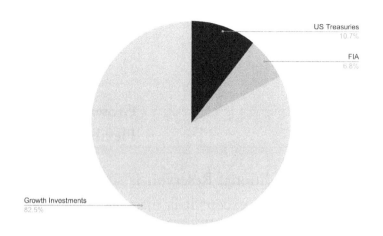

US Treasuries
10.7%

FIA
6.8%

Growth Investments
82.5%

Hypothetical illustration shown for demonstration purposes only. It is not guaranteed and not indicative of your actual plan results.

This type of reservoir may completely dry up earlier than expected in retirement. If that happens, you will need to refill it with the same or different investments or products. As you age, some products may not be available to you. Make sure you spend time vetting each of the options that could work at your current age and in the future.

The Larger-Ladder Reservoir

If your results were protection and structure, then the Larger-Ladder Reservoir may be right for you. Here's what it would look like on the chart.

	Structure	Flexibility
Protection	Protection + Structure	

Growth Potential

The Larger-Ladder Reservoir is intended to have a high amount of predictability for the first 20 years or so in retirement. Basically, regardless of market conditions, your income is expected to come from your Principal Guaranteed Reservoir™. Let's take a look at the example plan again.

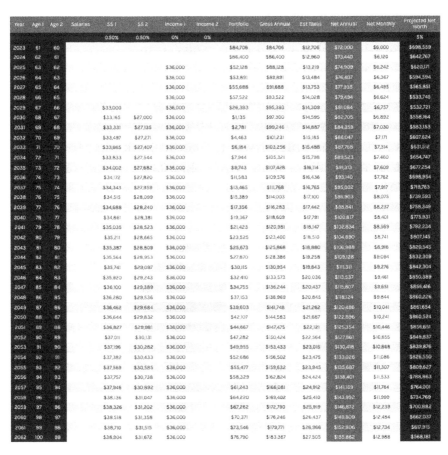

Year	Age 1	Age 2	Salaries	SS 1	SS 2	Income 1	Income 2	Portfolio	Gross Annual	Est Taxes	Net Annual	Net Monthly	Projected Net Worth
			0.50%	0.50%		0%	0%						5%
2023	61	60						$84,706	$84,706	$12,706	$72,000	$6,000	$698,559
2024	62	61						$86,400	$86,400	$12,960	$73,440	$6,120	$642,767
2025	63	62				$36,000		$52,128	$88,128	$13,219	$74,909	$6,242	$620,171
2026	64	63				$36,000		$53,891	$89,891	$13,484	$76,407	$6,367	$594,594
2027	65	64				$36,000		$55,688	$91,688	$13,753	$77,935	$6,495	$565,851
2028	66	65				$36,000		$57,522	$93,522	$14,028	$79,494	$6,624	$533,745
2029	67	66	$33,000			$36,000		$26,393	$95,393	$14,309	$81,084	$6,757	$532,721
2030	68	67	$33,165	$27,000		$36,000		$1,135	$97,300	$14,595	$82,705	$6,892	$558,164
2031	69	68	$33,331	$27,135		$36,000		$2,781	$99,246	$14,887	$84,358	$7,030	$583,153
2032	70	69	$33,497	$27,271		$36,000		$4,463	$101,231	$15,185	$86,047	$7,171	$607,624
2033	71	70	$33,865	$27,407		$36,000		$6,184	$103,256	$15,488	$87,768	$7,314	$631,512
2034	72	71	$33,833	$27,544		$36,000		$7,944	$105,321	$15,798	$89,523	$7,460	$654,747
2035	73	72	$34,002	$27,682		$36,000		$8,743	$107,428	$16,114	$91,313	$7,609	$677,254
2036	74	73	$34,172	$27,820		$36,000		$11,583	$109,576	$16,436	$93,140	$7,762	$698,954
2037	75	74	$34,343	$27,959		$36,000		$13,465	$111,768	$16,765	$95,002	$7,917	$719,763
2038	76	75	$34,515	$28,099		$36,000		$15,389	$114,003	$17,100	$96,903	$8,075	$739,593
2039	77	76	$34,688	$28,240		$36,000		$17,356	$116,283	$17,442	$98,841	$8,237	$758,348
2040	78	77	$34,861	$28,381		$36,000		$19,367	$118,608	$17,781	$100,817	$8,401	$775,931
2041	79	78	$35,035	$28,523		$36,000		$21,423	$120,981	$18,147	$102,834	$8,569	$792,234
2042	80	79	$35,211	$28,665		$36,000		$23,525	$123,400	$18,510	$104,890	$8,741	$807,145
2043	81	80	$35,387	$28,809		$36,000		$25,673	$125,868	$18,880	$106,988	$8,916	$820,545
2044	82	81	$35,564	$28,953		$36,000		$27,870	$128,386	$19,258	$109,128	$9,084	$832,309
2045	83	82	$35,741	$29,097		$36,000		$30,115	$130,954	$19,643	$111,311	$9,276	$842,304
2046	84	83	$35,920	$29,243		$36,000		$32,410	$133,573	$20,036	$113,537	$9,461	$850,389
2047	85	84	$36,100	$29,389		$36,000		$34,755	$136,244	$20,437	$115,807	$9,651	$856,416
2048	86	85	$36,280	$29,536		$36,000		$37,153	$138,968	$20,845	$118,124	$9,844	$860,226
2049	87	86	$36,462	$29,684		$36,000		$39,603	$141,748	$21,262	$120,486	$10,041	$861,654
2050	88	87	$36,644	$29,832		$36,000		$42,107	$144,583	$21,687	$122,896	$10,241	$860,524
2051	89	88	$36,827	$29,981		$36,000		$44,867	$147,475	$22,121	$125,354	$10,446	$856,651
2052	90	89	$37,011	$30,131		$36,000		$47,282	$150,424	$22,564	$127,861	$10,655	$849,837
2053	91	90	$37,196	$30,282		$36,000		$49,955	$153,433	$23,015	$130,418	$10,868	$839,876
2054	92	91	$37,382	$30,433		$36,000		$52,686	$156,502	$23,475	$133,026	$11,086	$826,550
2055	93	92	$37,569	$30,585		$36,000		$55,477	$159,632	$23,945	$135,687	$11,307	$809,627
2056	94	93	$37,757	$30,738		$36,000		$58,329	$162,824	$24,424	$138,401	$11,533	$788,863
2057	95	94	$37,946	$30,892		$36,000		$61,243	$166,081	$24,912	$141,169	$11,764	$764,001
2058	96	95	$38,136	$31,047		$36,000		$64,220	$169,402	$25,410	$143,992	$11,999	$734,769
2059	97	96	$38,326	$31,202		$36,000		$67,262	$172,790	$25,919	$146,872	$12,239	$700,882
2060	98	97	$38,518	$31,358		$36,000		$70,371	$176,246	$26,437	$149,809	$12,484	$662,037
2061	99	98	$38,710	$31,515		$36,000		$73,546	$179,771	$26,966	$152,806	$12,734	$617,915
2062	100	99	$38,904	$31,672		$36,000		$76,790	$183,367	$27,505	$155,862	$12,958	$568,181

Hypothetical illustration shown for demonstration purposes only. It is not guaranteed and not indicative of your actual plan results.

In order to design the Larger-Ladder Reservoir, you would need to use the investments and products that qualify for the Principal Guaranteed Reservoir™ and ladder them out based on their maturities or surrender schedules. As a reminder, those investment and product options are U.S. Treasuries, CDs, Fixed and Fixed-Indexed Annuities, and Cash Value Life Insurance.

What you use is up to you. Each option has its own benefits and detriments. It is common to use a little of each option, though. For example, you may pull income from U.S. Treasuries for years one and two. Then, in years 3, 4, and 5, you may consider laddering out CDs. Next, from years 6 to 10, you may consider fixed-indexed annuities. Lastly, between years 11 and 20, you may either only use fixed-indexed annuities or a blend of fixed-indexed annuities and cash value life insurance. This is just an example of what it could look like. If we were to look at these investments from the pie chart perspective, it would look something like this:

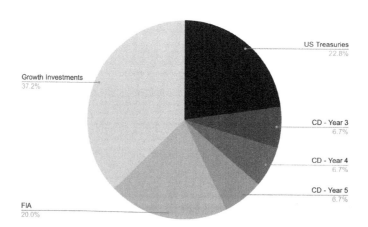

Hypothetical illustration shown for demonstration purposes only. It is not guaranteed and not indicative of your actual plan results.

Once 20 years are up, if implemented correctly, there should be some of your Principal Guaranteed Reservoir™ left over and liquid to help support you for the remainder of the plan.

Typically, someone who wants less risk and more structure would consider the Larger-Laddered Reservoir.

The Smaller-Ladder Reservoir

The Smaller-Ladder Reservoir consists of the same concept, only the ladder lasts for the first five years or so. Once the ladder ends, the portfolio then becomes the more traditional version of the Principal Guaranteed Reservoir™, only providing income when markets go down.

This portfolio design is typically better suited for someone who wants to front-load their plan and travel. Those first few years are important to the plan and the portfolio. As the Principle of Income suggests, you never want to pull income from accounts that have experienced significant losses. Instead of putting that kind of pressure on the portfolio, you may consider laddering out your income needs during the first few years, just in case a multi-year market crash occurs.

Here is an example of what it could look like from the pie chart perspective:

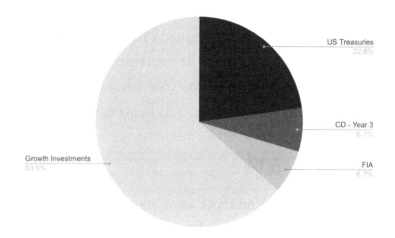

US Treasuries
22.8%

CD - Year 3
6.7%

FIA
6.7%

Growth Investments
63.9%

Hypothetical illustration shown for demonstration purposes only. It is not guaranteed and not indicative of your actual plan results.

Make sure to leave extra assets in the Principal Guaranteed Reservoir™ so that you can keep income coming in, even when markets crash, later in the plan. In other words, once the Smaller-Ladder has been completed, you still need to have something in your reservoir for when the markets crash later in the plan. It could end up looking like a Smaller Traditional Reservoir after year five or so.

In Conclusion

Finding your design is only the first step. In the next chapter, we are going to walk through a special way to review your assets and see what you are working with. My intention is to open your eyes and help you evaluate your portfolio differently than you may be used to doing.

I'll see you in the next chapter.

Chapter 10

THE PORTFOLIO ALIGNMENT ASSESSMENT

"You cannot rise higher than your foundation allows."

– Mike Decker

This will likely be the most important chapter in the entire book.

Why?

Because of something called the Dunning-Kruger Effect. Simply put, the Dunning-Kruger Effect explains why people tend to overestimate their own abilities. It's so easy to have high expectations, especially after a few good years in the market. It's not just your average investor who suffers from the Dunning-Kruger Effect. Financial professionals are guilty of it as well.

Greed is a powerful emotion. I do not want you to fall victim to these emotion-based traps. Remember, I want to help you.

Once you create your plan and you pick which type of Principal Guaranteed Reservoir™ you want, based on the assessments and explanations in the last chapter, you should be ready to compare what you need with how your portfolio is currently allocated. We want to use what you already have, as best as we can.

It's time to jump in and run an assessment, based on your current portfolio. Basically, we are looking to see how much you have at risk (growth potential with liquidity), how much you have in products that can be used as a Principal Guaranteed Reservoir™ (growth potential and protection), and how much you have in cash (liquid with protection).

Take a moment and fill out the graphic below. We are only looking for the current cash value of each investment or product. For example, if you have term life insurance, the cash value is $0. If you had cash value life insurance, it would be the total cash value amount, not your death benefit. Stocks, ETFs, Mutual Funds, and so on would be based on current market value. Use the descriptions on the left to organize which investments would go where on the chart.

Total
Value

Liquid & Principal Protected (Checking, Savings, Money Market, etc.)

Growth Potential & Principal Protected
(U.S. Treasuries, CDs, Fixed or Fixed-Indexed
Annuities, Cash Value Life Insurance)

Growth Potential & Liquid (Stocks, Mutual
Funds, ETFs, Variable Annuities, etc.)

If you have more than 6 months of income in the first group, the liquid and principal protected group, you may have too much allocated into accounts that tend to struggle keeping up with inflation. They say cash is king when markets go down, and cash is trash when markets go up. You cannot time the market. It's worth asking the question, "Why do you have so much in cash?" If you are waiting for the markets to turn around and start going up, you may have missed the point of the Principal Guaranteed Reservoir™.

Speaking of which, let's address the second group, growth potential and principal protected investments and products. This group represents your Principal Guaranteed Reservoir™. This is what is supposed to give you comfort and protection while you enjoy its growth potential.

If the number in this second group is less than the number you calculated in the exercise before, based on the portfolio design you picked (e.g., Smaller Traditional Reservoir, Larger Traditional Reservoir, Larger-Ladder Reservoir, and Smaller-Ladder Reservoir) then chances are you're taking too much risk. There may be some adjustments that need to be made for this to be set up correctly.

If you need more allocated in that group, consider adding U.S. Treasuries, CDs, Fixed or Fixed-Indexed Annuities, or Cash Value Life Insurance. If you want to consider Fixed or Fixed-Indexed Annuities, or Cash Value Life Insurance, you will need to go through a licensed insurance agent. I would recommend you work through someone who is independent and does research on rates and current offerings (like what we do at Kedrec).

Moving on, the last group, which represents your investments that traditionally have the highest growth potential, is whatever is left over. These investments are intended to help you keep up with inflation while potentially growing fast enough to help support you and your needs later in the plan.

So, how did you do?

Do you have a reservoir big enough to support you and the lifestyle you want?

If you need to make some adjustments, that's okay. That's the point of this exercise. We don't want to assume everything will magically work itself out. We also don't want to base our entire future on our ability to outsmart the market. Just like you have flashlights around the house for when the lights go out (or a generator), you have a reservoir for when the markets go down.

The Basic Tax Assessment

Putting a portfolio together is more than a look at the investments themselves. There's another layer of complexity that many people miss. There are essentially three types of accounts your assets could be in; Pre-Tax accounts, After-Tax accounts, and Tax-Free accounts. Where your money is, based on these accounts, can have an impact on how you set up your portfolio. Before we go any further, please fill in the total values below based on how much you have in each tax category.

Total Value

Pre-Tax (401(k), IRA, 403(B), etc.)

After-Tax (brokerage account, checking/savings, etc.)

Tax-Free (Roth-IRAs, cash value life insurance, etc.)

If the majority of your assets are in the pre-tax bucket, taxes will most likely be a problem that needs to be addressed. If taxes go up, your overall income could go down. That's a problem. In order to address this potential problem, it may take several years of planning and execution. As the expression goes, the only way to eat an elephant is one bite at a time.

If you are actively trading in your account, and/or using dividend-based investments in your after-tax accounts, short-term capital gains may be an issue in retirement. Sure, anytime you pay short-term capital gains, you are making money. However, it could stunt other tax-minimization strategies, ultimately making the overall tax-minimization effort less efficient. There's no such thing as a perfect investment strategy. We want to do what we can to help ensure that the multiple strategies implemented do not conflict with each other.

In Conclusion

As we wrap up, I want to mention that this assessment is an oversimplified exercise intended to help put the big picture into perspective while connecting a few dots. Please be mindful that you will most likely feel a bias towards what you have currently allocated in your portfolio. It is familiar, and we as humans tend to prefer what is familiar. Just because it may be familiar doesn't mean it is right, it just means that it is familiar.

If you want a more in-depth analysis, consider booking a call with my team and requesting a more in-depth Wealth Blind Spots Assessment by going to www.kedrec.com/call.

They do this day-in and day-out.

We want to help people, like you, make principle-based decisions.

We are almost done.

I'll see you in the conclusion section.

Conclusion

CREATING YOUR DREAM RETIREMENT

WHAT TO DO NEXT

W e've reached the end of the book, but the start of something incredible. I sincerely hope that you've been able to gain the knowledge needed to retire on time with a plan designed to last longer than you.

Here's a quick recap of what we've covered:

1. Retirees have more than market crashes to worry about. From flat market cycles to taxes possibly going up, and much more. Retirement success doesn't happen by accident.

2. Common income strategies, like the 4% Rule or annuitized income annuities, have more risk potential than people realize. It is important to avoid extremes like having all of your assets at risk or all of your assets locked up in income annuities.

3. The Principle of Income suggests that you **only draw retirement income from accounts that have not received significant losses.** Failing to do so may have negative effects on your income and assets and may ultimately compromise your retirement.

4. The Principle of Diversification suggests that you **diversify your assets by objectives** instead of lumping everything together with investment ambiguity. Once you retire, your assets have additional responsibilities that must be accounted for.

5. The Principle of Planning suggests that **predetermined guidelines increase your probability of future success**. Failing to set guidelines can lead to a reactive future and eventually compromise your retirement.

6. The Principal Guaranteed Reservoir™ strategy suggests that you fund a portion of your portfolio in investments or products that cannot lose money (e.g., U.S. Treasuries if held to maturity, CDs, fixed and fixed-indexed annuities if not annuitized, and cash value life insurance if the fees make sense).

7. **There's no such thing as a perfect investment.**

8. There's no such thing as a perfect investment strategy.

9. Plan before you talk about products or strategies. You need your plan in order to have context.

10. Any plan you create will need to be maintained. No one knows what the future holds, but when you follow principles, you put probability on your side.

11. As you maintain your Functional Wealth Plan™, it is important to stick to the principles. Don't get greedy. Markets go up and down. Just because they may go up in the beginning doesn't mean they will always go up. A Functional Wealth Plan™, when built correctly, is designed to last longer than you. That assumes it is being funded and maintained correctly.

The next step is simple.

Start.

If you haven't yet, go to the website and create your preliminary Functional Wealth Plan™.

www.kedrec.com/plan

All of your information is anonymous unless you decide to submit your results and schedule a call with my team.

At that point, you can decide if you want help from my team of financial planners and tax professionals or if you want to go it alone.

Either way, start.

Make one small decision, then take one small step.

Your Functional Wealth Plan™ isn't created by accident. Chances are, your assets are still allocated the same as when you were working. The transition to a proper retirement portfolio that is designed to support you throughout retirement doesn't happen overnight. It takes careful and thoughtful planning accompanied by the correct strategies.

A Functional Wealth Plan™ may not be able to help you retire today, but it might show you how to retire sooner than expected.

First, though, you have to start.

Run the numbers.

If you decide to schedule a call, there are a few things to understand.

At any point during the call, it is okay to say no.

We only work with people who want to work with us.

We are not a fit for everyone, and that's okay.

That being said, if you want to have a conversation with my team, schedule a call by using the URL below.

www.kedrec.com/call

We're good at what we do.

To your retirement success,

MIKE DECKER

BONUSES

This book contains a significant amount of bonuses when purchased. We didn't get a chance to dive deep into important topics, which is why the bonus material exists. If you want to access your bonus content, you'll need to go to edu.kedrec.com and log in.

Once you log in, you should find the digital copy of this book, the audiobook, and much more.

If you purchased this book on Amazon or another book retailer, you would need to send an email to support@kedrec.com with the subject line "Requesting Bonus Access." Once we receive it, we will grant access to the email that was used. You should expect to gain access within one business day.

One of the major bonuses that you can access right now is the Functional Wealth Calculator. As a reminder, you can access that calculator by going to www.kedrec.com/plan.

If you have any trouble accessing your bonuses, please contact support@kedrec.com.

Also, as promised, if you need to find more information about your Social Security benefit, go to www.ssa.gov, create an account, and pull your numbers.

HOW TO GET MORE HELP

We love helping people transition into retirement with a plan that is designed to last longer than them. We also love working with people who have already retired, but feel that they need a different plan.

This book covered how to create a broad-based plan. There's a lot we just could not cover, for one reason or another. If we were sitting in a room together, discussing your retirement, here are all the other things I would have loved to discuss with you.

- Enhanced income planning, like adjusting income based on your mortgage payoff date, how Medicare affects your budget, and so on.
- How to prepare now to transition into retirement late.
- Uncommon strategies that can help you prepare for retirement.
- Alternative investment options for those who want more diversification.
- Why budgets fail and how Functional Cashflow™ can help.
- Understanding when to keep debt, and when to just pay it off.
- Advanced tax minimization strategies.
- Advanced tax planning strategies within your Functional Wealth Plan™.
- Legacy portfolio creation.
- Legacy planning strategies.

- Estate document creation/updates.
- Pension analysis.
- Social Security optimization.
- Medicare/Medicaid planning.
- Advanced healthcare planning.
- Required Minimum Distribution (RMD) preparation and planning.
- Retirement Transition Coaching (Emotional Intelligence).
- And more.

Everything above has many variables and exceptions. Unless we are having a conversation, it becomes extremely difficult to offer guidance. This is why we offer our comprehensive planning services. Here's how it works.

We charge a one-time fee for up to five 60–90-minute planning sessions. Our mission is to create a retirement plan that is designed to last longer than you, and is easy enough to manage that once we are done, you can manage it on your own.

Once the plan is done, you can manage your plan and your investments on your own, or manage your plan on your own while we professionally manage your investments with our Probability Investment Models™, or you could have us manage everything (like a family office, if you know what that is).

There's a good chance that we could help you further increase your growth potential and help decrease your overall risk.

If you want to learn more, schedule a call.

We want to help.

www.kedrec.com/call

ABOUT THE AUTHOR

Mike Decker started his financial career in 2013. He was originally hired to help with marketing but was quickly tasked with rebuilding and improving the firm's planning software and general firm operations. It wasn't long before he was promoted to run the operations of this firm.

Years later, he left to help create another financial practice that experienced significant success in the retirement space. Once that practice grew to a certain point, he made his exit and went out on his own.

Mike founded Kedrec with the intention of making things right in the financial space. He fully acknowledges that the financial services space (namely stockbrokers and insurance agents) is among the most distrusted professions according to Gallup reports[5], and he is committed to making things right. Mike is motivated to do what is right for the client.

Over the years, Mike has been recognized as an influential national coach to other financial advisors. His work has been featured in major publications, such as MarketWatch, Yahoo! Finance, Fox News, CBS, MSNBC, and other major publications. He currently contributes on a regular basis to Kiplinger.

When Mike's not in the office, he's focused on spending time with his family. Odds are, he's either cooking something special on his Big Green Egg®, playing improvised blues with one of the many instruments he's learned over the years, or on a mountain with his skies or mountain bike, depending on the season.

All inquiries for podcast appearances, video shows, and speaking can be sent to info@kedrec.com.

DISCLOSURE

Investing involves risk, including the potential loss of principal. No investment strategy can guarantee a profit or protect against loss in periods of declining values. None of the information contained in this book shall constitute an offer to sell or solicit any offer to buy a security or any insurance product. This book should not be construed as tax, legal, or investment advice.

The purpose of this book is to provide general information on the subjects discussed. It is not intended to be used as the sole basis for financial decisions, nor should it be construed as advice designed to meet the particular needs of an individual's situation. Insurance product guarantees are backed by the financial strength and claims-paying ability of the issuing company.

Life insurance and annuity products are not FDIC-insured. Product and feature availability may vary by state.

NOTES

[1] Not representative of all retirees. The strategies outlined in this book offer no guarantee as to your own financial success.

[2] Sean Williams, "The 3 Most Important Stock Market Crash Statistics You'll Ever See," The Motley Fool, Oct. 10, 2020, https://www.fool.com/investing/2020/10/10/the-3-most-important-stock-market-crash-statistics/

[3] Mark Kolakowski, "A Brief History of U.S. Bear Markets, Investopedia.com, Sept. 23, 2022, https://www.investopedia.com/a-history-of-bear-markets-4582652 and Paul Kaplan, "In Long History of Market Crashes, Coronavirus Crash Was the Shortest," Morningstar.com, Mar. 9, 2021, https://www.morningstar.com/articles/1028407/in-long-history-of-market-crashes-coronavirus-crash-was-the-shortest

[4] Dr. Robert Shiller, Online Data Robert Shiller, http://www.econ.yale.edu/~shiller/data.htm

[5] Sarah Cunnane, "Americans say these are the most dishonest professions", Moneywise.com, December 2021, https://moneywise.com/life/entertainment/americans-say-these-are-the-most-dishonest-professions

Made in the USA
Middletown, DE
05 November 2023

41987283R00099